Getting Ready for Speech

A Beginner's Guide to Public Speaking

by
Charles LeBeau & David Harrington

Published by Language Solutions Incorporated
* 1316 Mount Pitt Avenue * Medford, Oregon * 97501 * USA *
Phone: 1-877-526-4765 *
www.languagesolutionsinc.com
information@languagesolutionsinc.com

Book Design: Language Solutions/David Harrington/Hiroaki Udo
Production: Language Solutions
Layout: Hiroaki Udo
Design: Hiroaki Udo/Chidori Ando/Kazumi Nagano/Mami Harrington
Front Cover Illustration: Ty Semaka
Inside Illustrations: Ty Semaka/Hiroaki Udo
Copyediting: Chris Bartlett
Voice Actors: Michael S. Arrington, Florian Grabis, Shallon K. Hanson, David Harrington, Charles LeBeau, Jack Merluzzi, Dana Robello, John Storm, James Vagasky, Judy Venable, and Amy Yagi.
Clip Art: Corel Draw

Every effort has been made to contact all of the copyright holders, if any have been inadvertantly overlooked the publishers will be pleased to make the necessary arrangements at the first opportunity.

Student Book........ISBN 1-929274-49-1
Student Book with English-Japanese glossary
..........................ISBN 1-929274-45-9
Audio Cassette.....ISBN 1-929274-46-7
Audio CD...............ISBN 1-929274-47-5

Printed and bound in Singapore
10 9 8 7 6 5 4 3 2 1

Clarke

Dear Teachers,

When we finished writing our first book in April of 1996 we worried. We worried whether there was a market for a low-level book on presentation. We worried whether you would like the illustrations and format. We worried whether anybody but our relatives would even buy the book!

To our great joy, our first book was received by you with open arms. Over the past few years we have been thrilled to talk to many of you in person about your experience using it in the classroom. We have listened to your feedback and have come back to you with a new offering, Getting Ready For Speech, an even lower level speech book. We have tried to keep what you liked best and improve the rest.
Thank you all for your comments.

This book is for you.

Acknowledgments:

Charles and David would like to thank: The people at The English Resource; Michio Abe, Miyoko Abe, Chidori Ando, Miho Amemiya, Chris Bartlett, Tomoko Bartlett, Dana Chaffin, Akiko Fujita, Tatsuya Fukuyama, Mami Harrington, Hatsumi Kiryu, Megumi Nakada, Nobumichi Nishimura, Noriko Ogawa, Yoko Terada, Koji Yamamoto and Mieko Yoshinaga. The people at I.P.I. Raphael Bourgeois, Reiko Hisatake, Kazumi Nagano, AtsuhikoTada. The teachers who encourage and inspire us; Carl Adams, Tim Allen, Graham Bathgate, Bruce Davidson, Joseph Dilenschneider, Don Hinkleman, Brent Jones, Keith Lane, John McLaughlin, Allan Murphy, Rieko Nagamasa, Sophia Shang, Joe Tomei, and the many other teachers who have helped us over the years.

Charles LeBeau would like to thank: My life support system (Bill, Michael, Yuko, Sal, Pat, Bob, Frank, and Bud) for their unswerving loyalty, encouragement, and faith. All of the brilliant staff at Language Solutions. And most of all my family (Nobuko, Ray, Jay, my mother, and my brothers).

David Harrington would like to thank: Mami Ushida Harrington, Kikiyo Marie Harrington and Tsukasa James Harrington for teaching me what love has to do with it. My family Becky, Dick, Nan, Trudy, Hatsue Ushida and all their families for their love and support. Those wonderful people I call friends; Masami & Kaori, Kagetora, Ginpei, Keiko, Hiroko & Joe, Minako & Takeshi, Shane & Carolyn, Jason & Tomomi, Ash, Suwa, Azam, Hiroko, Chidori, Kazumi, Masumi, Tomoko, Pat, Jeff, Lisa, Yuka, Mayela, Daniel, Elsa, Dayel, Pancho and Tanuki Master Satoru. I love you all.

Table of Contents

Table of Contents

To the Teacher

Thanks to your input, we have identified 7 types of speeches you would like your students to experience:

1. Self-Introduction Speeches
2. Introducing Someone
3. Demonstration Speeches
4. Layout Speeches
5. Book and Movie Reviews
6. Show and Tell
7. Presenting and Accepting Awards

Each of the seven units in *Getting Ready for Speech* targets one of these speeches. Each unit empowers the learner with the language and speech skills necessary to successfully do the target speech by the end of the unit. To this end, each unit walks the students through six steps: Model, Language, Delivery, Practice, Final Speech and Structure.

MODEL The Model presents short recorded samples of the unit's target speech. A simple listening task focuses the learner's attention on the key language and components of the target speech.

LANGUAGE The Language section highlights the grammar focus and expressions of the Model speeches. With the use of visual prompts, students practice these basic patterns through interactive recorded drills.

DELIVERY The Delivery section of each unit focuses on a different aspect of the "physical message." We have responded to you and your students' enthusiasm for the physical message by expanding it into a full section in each unit.

PRACTICE The Practice section integrates language and delivery in a task recycled from the Model section. Whereas in the Model section students listened to the tape to complete the task, here students listen to a partner to complete the task.

SPEECH The Final Speech is the culmination of the unit. Learners plug their own experience into the components of the target speech and then deliver their speech to a partner, to a group, or to the class.

STRUCTURE The Structure section is a final review of the language and grammar of the unit. It can be done in class or assigned as homework. This section can also be done immediately following the Language section to reinforce the basic patterns of the unit.

Getting Ready for Speech is supported by the Internet. For a free downloadable copy of the tape script and the Teacher's Notes, please visit www.languagesolutionsinc.com. Moreover, throughout the book, we have placed Internet icons to indicate interesting links for reference and research. To locate these sites visit our homepage, www.languagesolutionsinc.com. Finally, we would love to hear from you. Drop us a line at information@languagesolutionsinc.com.

Peace, Love, and Happiness always,
Charles and David
(The guys who wrote this book)

~ Introduction Speeches ~

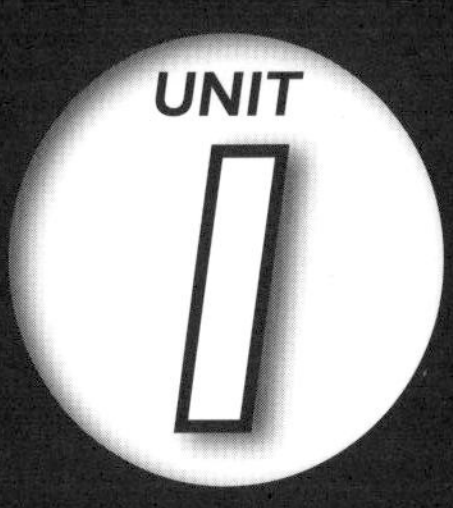

Self-introduction

ABOUT THIS UNIT

Goal	Introduce yourself in a confident, interesting manner
Key Language	I live in ~ My hobby is ~ I hope to ~
Delivery Focus	Posture
Final Speech	Give a self-introduction Speech in front of the class

Listen to the three self-introduction speeches. Complete the tables. The first one is done for you.

Track 2

Listening 1

Hello everyone!
My name is Suzie Chang.
I was born in San Francisco.
I'm studying art.
In my free time, I enjoy drawing and painting.
Someday, I hope to study at the Art Institute of Chicago.
Thank you.

Name	Suzie Chang
Birthplace	San Francisco
School / Work	art
Free Time	draw and paint
Hopes & Dreams	study at A.I.C.

Track 3

Listening 2

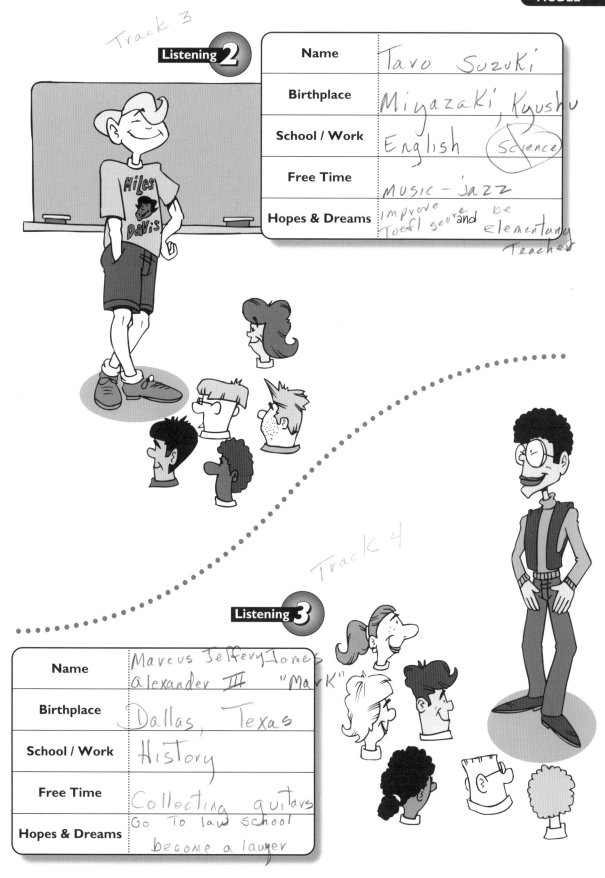

Name	Taro Suzuki
Birthplace	Miyazaki, Kyushu
School / Work	English (Science)
Free Time	music - jazz
Hopes & Dreams	improve Toefl score and be elementary Teacher

Track 4

Listening 3

Name	Marcus Jeffery Jones alexander III "Mark"
Birthplace	Dallas, Texas
School / Work	History
Free Time	Collecting guitars
Hopes & Dreams	Go To law school become a lawyer

Self-introduction Speech

Study these expressions for self-introduction speeches.

Greeting:	**Hello everyone!** **Good morning!** **Hi!**
Name:	**My name is** Suzie Chang. **I'm** Taro Suzuki. **My name is** Marcus Jeffery James Alexander III, **but you can call me** Mark.
Birthplace:	**I was born in** San Francisco. **I'm from** Miyazaki, Kyushu. **My hometown is** Dallas, Texas.
School or Work:	**I'm studying** art. At school, **I'm good at** English, but **I'm not very good at** science. **My favorite subject is** history.
Free time:	**In my free time, I enjoy** drawing and painting. **I like** listening to music, particularly jazz. **My hobby is** collecting guitars.
Hopes and Dreams:	**Someday, I hope to** study at the Art Institute of Chicago. **I would like to** improve my TOEFL score. **I want to** be an elementary school teacher. **My dream is to** go to law school and become a lawyer.
Closing:	**Thank you!** **Thanks for listening.** **Thank you for your attention.**

How to Use the Language Page.

The language pages are filled with the basic words and phrases you need to make the speeches in this book. Notice that some words are in **bold type** and some words are not. The words in **bold** are whole phrases that you can use to make your speeches by just adding your own information.

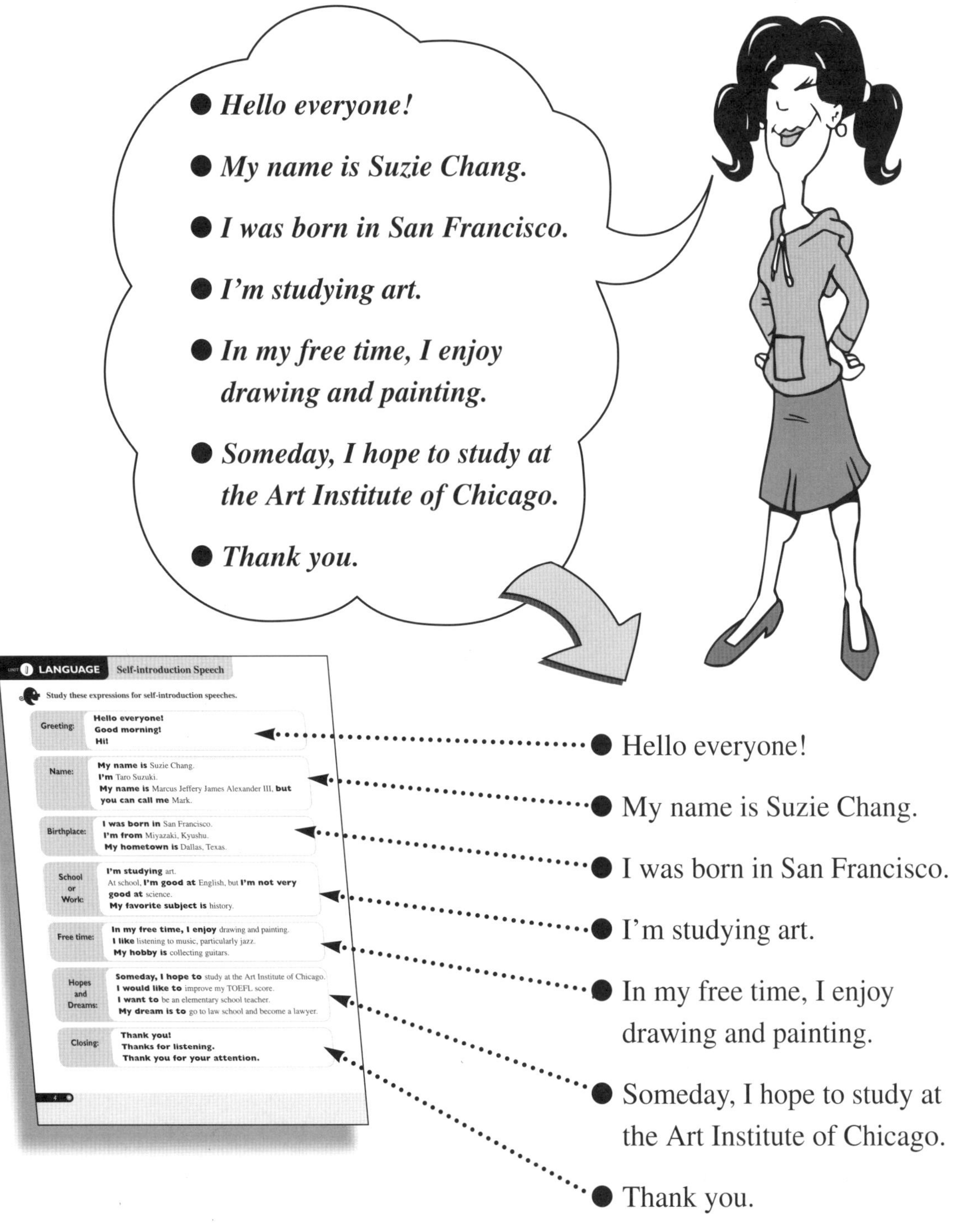
Hello everyone!
My name is Suzie Chang.
I was born in San Francisco.
I'm studying art.
In my free time, I enjoy drawing and painting.
Someday, I hope to study at the Art Institute of Chicago.
Thank you.
UNIT 1 LANGUAGE Self-introduction Speech
Study these expressions for self-introduction speeches.
Greeting: Hello everyone! Good morning! Hi!
Name: My name is Suzie Chang. I'm Taro Suzuki. My name is Marcus Jeffery James Alexander III, but you can call me Mark.
Birthplace: I was born in San Francisco. I'm from Miyazaki, Kyushu. My hometown is Dallas, Texas.
School or Work: I'm studying art. At school, I'm good at English, but I'm not very good at science. My favorite subject is history.
Free time: In my free time, I enjoy drawing and painting. I like listening to music, particularly jazz. My hobby is collecting guitars.
Hopes and Dreams: Someday, I hope to study at the Art Institute of Chicago. I would like to improve my TOEFL score. I want to be an elementary school teacher. My dream is to go to law school and become a lawyer.
Closing: Thank you! Thanks for listening. Thank you for your attention.
4
Hello everyone!
My name is Suzie Chang.
I was born in San Francisco.
I'm studying art.
In my free time, I enjoy drawing and painting.
Someday, I hope to study at the Art Institute of Chicago.
Thank you.

How to Use the Language Practice Pages.

Step 1

Study the phrases on the Language Page.

Unit 1 LANGUAGE Self-introduction Speech

Study these expressions for self-introduction speeches.

Greeting:	**Hello everyone!** **Good morning!** **Hi!**
Name:	**My name is** Suzie Chang. **I'm** Taro Suzuki. **My name is** Marcus Jeffery James Alexander III, **but you can call me** Mark.
Birthplace:	**I was born in** San Francisco. **I'm from** Miyazaki, Kyushu. **My hometown is** Dallas, Texas.
School or Work:	**I'm studying** art. At school, **I'm good at** English, but **I'm not very good at** science. **My favorite subject is** history.
Free time:	**In my free time, I enjoy** drawing and painting. **I like** listening to music, particularly jazz. **My hobby is** collecting guitars.
Hopes and Dreams:	**Someday, I hope to** study at the Art Institute of Chicago. **I would like to** improve my TOEFL score. **I want to** be an elementary school teacher. **My dream is to** go to law school and become a lawyer.
Closing:	**Thank you!** **Thanks for listening.** **Thank you for your attention.**

Step 2

Look at the Practice Page and listen to the prompts.

born in New York.

Step 3

Say the full sentence using the words from the prompts and the patterns from the Language Page.

Step 4

Listen to the correct answer. How did you do?

I was born in New York.

Let's try! Listen and follow the instructions.

born in | from | hometown

1. New York
2. Moscow
3. Hong Kong

studying | good at | favorite subject

4. chemistry
5. music
6. math

like | hobby | enjoy

7. lifting weights
8. building model airplanes
9. reading

Study and practice these 4 easy steps for good speech posture.

Step 1 Set your posture.

Step 2 Set your hands.

Hint If you are speaking from notes, hold them quietly with both hands just about waist high.

Step 3

Look at your audience.

Step 4 Begin with a loud voice.

Practice getting ready to speak.

Walk to the front and set your posture and hands.

Round 1

The Speaker's Role:
All students stand in a line. Students take turns walking to the front, setting their posture, setting their hands, looking at the other students in the audience and greeting the audience in a loud presentation voice.

Look at the other students and greet them in a loud presentation voice.

Good morning!

Students stand in a line.

Round 2

The same as Round 1, but this time greet the audience AND give your name.

Round 3

The same as Round 2, but this time greet the audience, give your name AND your birthplace.

Change speaker.

Partner A looks at this page. Partner B looks at page 12.

Practice 1 **Read this self-introduction of a famous person. Your partner will try to guess who it is.**

Birthplace:

Hello everyone.
I'm from the Dominican Republic, a small Spanish speaking country in the Caribbean.
Now, I live in Chicago.

Work:

I also play ball in Chicago.
I bat right-handed and play in the outfield.
I am good at hitting home runs.
After I hit a homerun, I put 2 fingers on my heart and kiss them to the air.
It is my trademark.

Free time:

In my free time, I like playing with my children.
I like sailing my 60-foot yacht in the Caribbean, too.
My hobby is collecting cars.
I have 12.
I also do charity work.
Every year, I give $500,000 to schools in the Dominican Republic.

Hopes and Dreams:

Someday, I hope to win a World Series.
After I retire, I want to spend more time with my family.

Closing:

Thank you for your attention.

Name:

Who am I?

Answer on Page 15

Practice 2 **Now, listen to your partner read the self-introduction of another famous person. Fill out the table and guess who it is.**

Birthplace	
Work	
Free Time	
Hopes & Dreams	
Name	

Who am I?

Partner B looks at this page. Partner A looks at page 10.

Practice 1 **Listen to your partner read the self-introduction of a famous person. Fill out the table and guess who it is.**

Birthplace	
Work	
Free Time	
Hopes & Dreams	
Name	

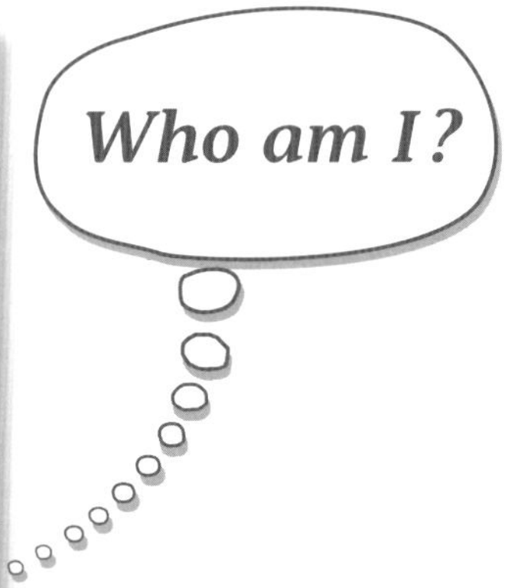

Who am I?

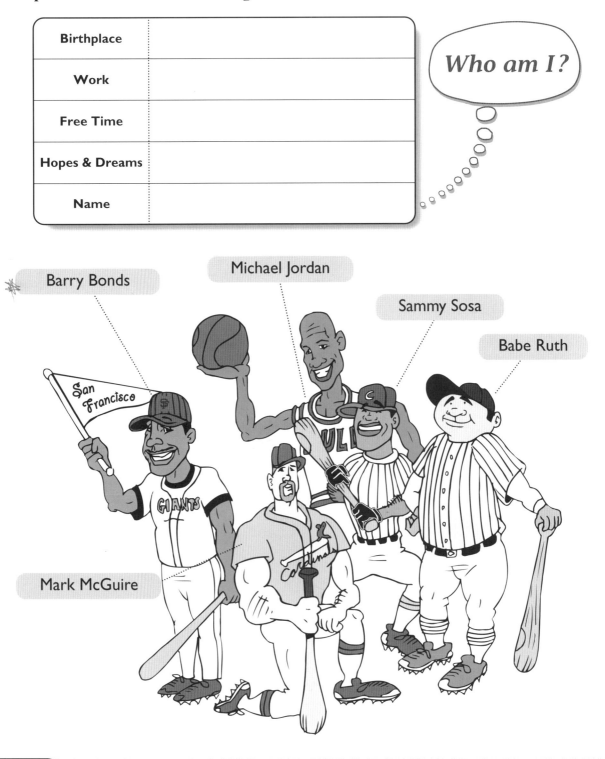

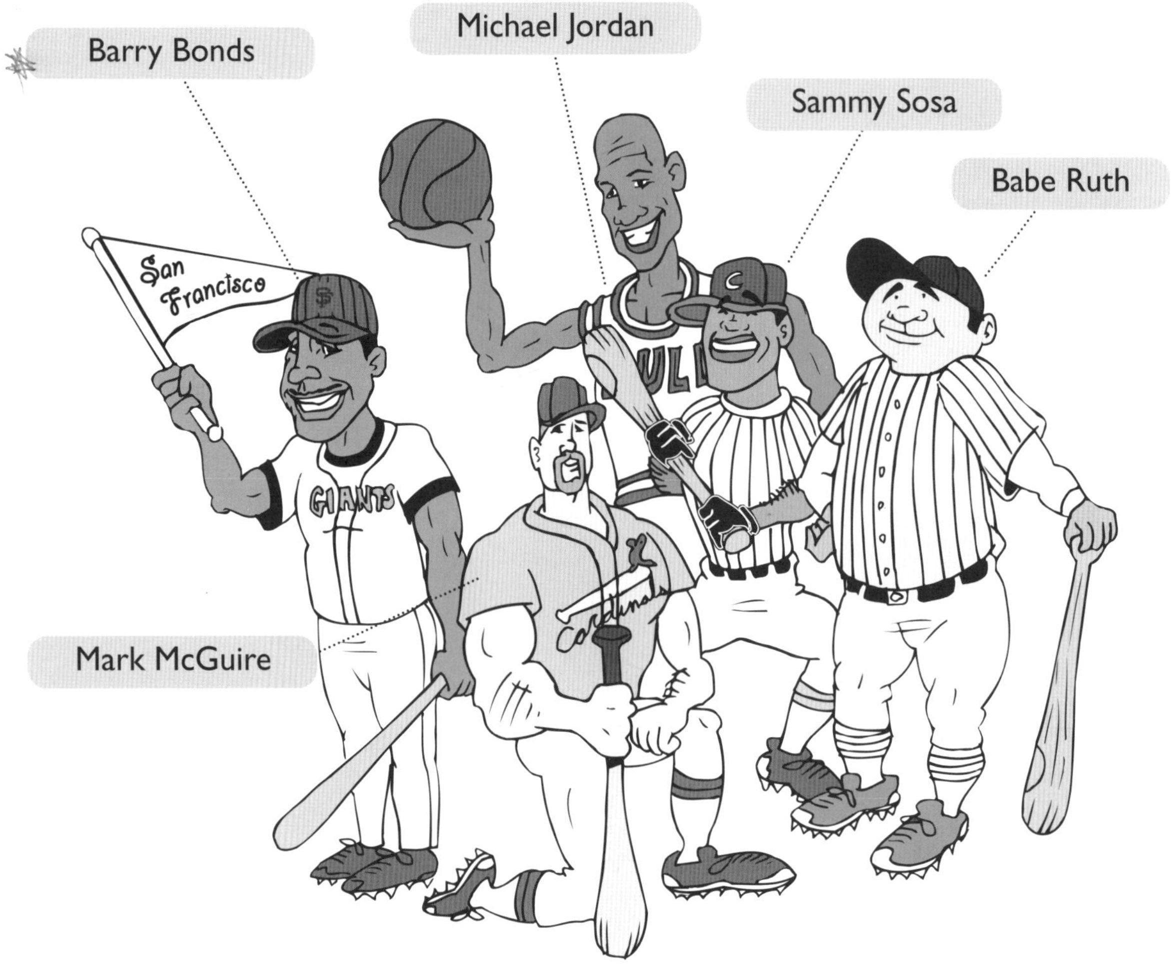

Barry Bonds

Michael Jordan

Sammy Sosa

Babe Ruth

Mark McGuire

Practice 2 **Read this self-introduction of a famous person. Your partner looks at page 11 and tries to guess who it is.**

Greetings:
Hi!

Birthplace:
I was born in Slovakia, but now my home is in Switzerland.

Work:
I'm good at tennis and I have won a lot of trophies.
My favorite trophy is the 1997 Wimbledon Women's Singles Trophy.
I am one of the youngest people ever to win a singles title at Wimbledon.

Free time:
In my free time, I like rollerblading.
I also like horseback riding.
I even have my own horse.
His name is Montana.

Hopes and Dreams:
I would like to keep playing tennis for many more years.
I hope to play at Wimbledon again.
I want to win another Wimbledon title.
Did you know that I was even named after a famous Wimbledon champion?

Closing:
Thanks for listening.

Name:
Who am I?

Self-introduction Speech

Select from these phrases to make a self-introduction to your class:

Greeting:	**Hello everyone!** **Good morning!** **Hi!**
Name:	**My name is …** **I'm …** **My name is …, but you can call me …**
Birthplace:	**I was born in …** **I'm from …** **My hometown is …**
School or Work:	**I'm studying …** **I'm good at …** **I'm not very good at …** **My favorite subject is …**
Free time:	**In my free time, I enjoy …** **I like …** **My hobby is …**
Hopes and Dreams:	**Someday, I hope to …** **I would like to …** **I want to …** **My dream is to …**
Closing:	**Thank you!** **Thanks for listening.** **Thank you for your attention.**

Make a self-introduction speech!

Greeting:
Hello everyone!
Good morning!
Hi!
Name:
My name is . . .
I'm . . .
My name is . . . , but . . .
you can call me . . .
I'm studying . . .
I'm good at . . .
I'm not very good at . . .
My favorite subject is . . .
In my free time, I enjoy . . .
I like . . .
My hobby is . . .
Hopes and Dreams:
Someday, I hope to . . .
I would like to . . .
I want to . . .
My dream is to . . .
Closing:
Thank you!
Thanks for listening.
Thank you for your attention.
Hello everyone!
SPEECH

Step 1 CHOOSE

Choose a phrase from page 14 for each of the speaking points.

Step 2 WRITE

Write the phrase and add your own personal information.

Step 3 SPEAK

Use this page to give your own self-introduction speech.

Speaking Points

Introduction

Greeting ______________________

Body

Name ______________________

Birthplace ______________________

School ______________________

Free time ______________________

Hopes & Dreams ______________________

Conclusion

Closing ______________________

UNIT 1 **STRUCTURE** **Basic Patterns**

Exercise 1 **The sentences in the following self-introduction speech are jumbled. Rewrite the corrected sentences on the lines below.**

① morning good
Good Morning !

② name is my Bruce Richardson
My name is .

③ hometown my Cleveland Ohio is
My hometown is , .

④ subject favorite journalism is my
My favorite subject is .

⑤ particularly sports basketball I like
I particularly like , .

⑥ medical school dream to my is doctor become a and go to
My dream is to go to medical school and become a doctor.

⑦ you thank
Thank you .

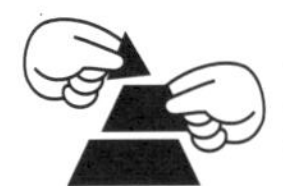

Exercise 2 **Fill in the blanks using the phrases you have learned.**

① My name is William Chang but you can call me Bill.

② I was born in Hong Kong but now I live in beautiful San Francisco.

③ I'm good at chemistry, but I'm not very good at French.

④ In my free time, I enjoy rollerblading and I also like skateboarding.

⑤ In this class, I would like to improve my speaking ability.

⑥ Thank you for listening.

Getting Ready for Speech

~ Introduction Speeches ~

UNIT 2

Introducing Someone

ABOUT THIS UNIT

Goal	Learn how to introduce someone to an audience
Key Language	He grew up in ~ She always/usually/sometimes ~
Delivery Focus	Eye contact
Final Speech	Introduce a classmate to the class

UNIT 2 MODEL Introducing Someone

Listen to speakers introducing Max Kandinsky, Ben Springer, and Ken Sato. Complete the tables.

Hello everyone!
This is our teacher,
Max Kandinsky.
Max teaches history and
art but he tells me his...

What is Max's favorite subject?	ART
Where is he from?	NY
Where does he live?	Oakland
What is his hometown famous for?	diversity of people & cultures
What does he do on the weekends?	Museums Libraries
What does he hope to do during his vacation?	Florence Italy

Listening 2

What is Ben's favorite subject?	Chinese
Where is he from?	Seattle
Where does he live?	
What is his hometown famous for?	Microsoft, Boeing, Starbucks
What does he do on the weekends?	tennis, go out
What does he hope to do during his vacation?	Parents in New Orleans

Listening 3

What is Ken's favorite subject?	Math
Where is he from?	Kumamoto
Where does he live?	L A
What is his hometown famous for?	castle
What does he do on the weekends?	sleeps, shops
What does he hope to do during his vacation?	Europe, motor

Introducing Someone

Study these expressions for speeches introducing someone.

Person's Name:	**This is our teacher,** Max Kandinsky. **This is my friend,** Ben Springer. **This is our classmate,** Ken Sato.
Favorite Subject:	**He tells me his favorite subject is** art. **He likes studying** Chinese. **His favorite subject is** math.
Hometown:	**He is originally from** New York. **He was raised in** Seattle. **He grew up in** Kumamoto.
Residence:	**He now lives over in** Oakland. **He still lives there.** **He now lives here in** L.A.
Hometown's Claim to Fame:	**He says** New York **is known for** the diversity of people and cultures. **He says that** Seattle **is famous for** three companies, Microsoft, Boeing, and Starbucks. **He says that** Kumamoto **has a** beautiful and historic castle.
Weekends:	**On the weekends, he usually** visits museums and libraries. **On Saturdays and Sundays, he sometimes** plays tennis or goes out with friends. **On his days off, he always** sleeps late, and he usually goes shopping in the afternoon.
Vacation Plans:	**He hopes to** go to Florence, Italy **during summer vacation**. **During his next vacation, he would like to** visit his parents in New Orleans. **This summer, he wants to** travel around Europe by motorcycle.
Closing:	**Please give him a warm welcome.** **Let's welcome him.** **Let's give him a warm welcome.**

Let's try! Listen and follow the instructions.

Always	Usually	Sometimes
1 	2 	3 
 [he] **go**	[she] **play**	[he] **practice**
4 	5 	6 
[they] **go**	[she] **play**	[he] **watch**
7 	8 	9 
 [they] **go**	[he] **play**	 [she] **bake**

Good eye contact is a 3-step process:

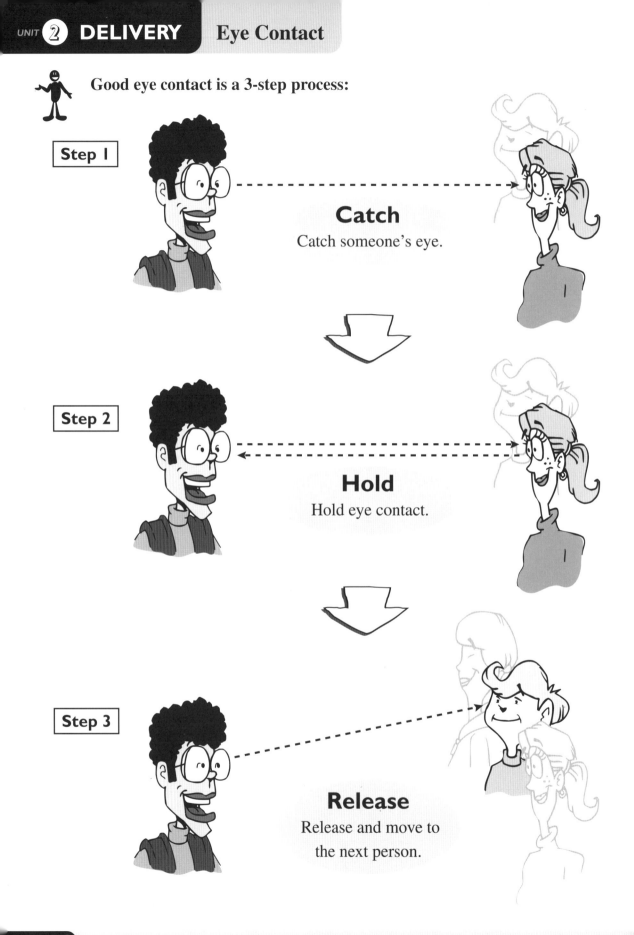

Step 1

Catch

Catch someone's eye.

Step 2

Hold

Hold eye contact.

Step 3

Release

Release and move to the next person.

Practice this eye contact game!

The Audience's Role:

When the speaker makes eye contact with you, raise your hand and keep it raised as long as the speaker is looking at you. When the speaker looks away, lower your hand.

Change speakers.

The Speaker's Role:

Practice catching, holding, and releasing eye contact. In a loud, clear presentation voice, say "catch, hold, release" as you look at each person in your group. Remember to get ready to speak: set your hands, look at the audience, and begin with a loud presentation voice.

Round 1

Walk to the front, set your posture and say "***catch, hold, release***" as you make eye contact.

Round 2

Repeat as in round 1, but this time count ***1-2-3*** to the first person, ***4-5-6*** to the second person, etc.

Round 3

Repeat as in round 1, but this time say the alphabet as you make eye contact with each person.

Goal **There must be one hand in the air at all times. If there isn't, it is a signal that the speaker has poor eye contact!**

Partner A looks at this page, partner B looks at page 25.

Practice 1 Interview your partner and write the answers below.

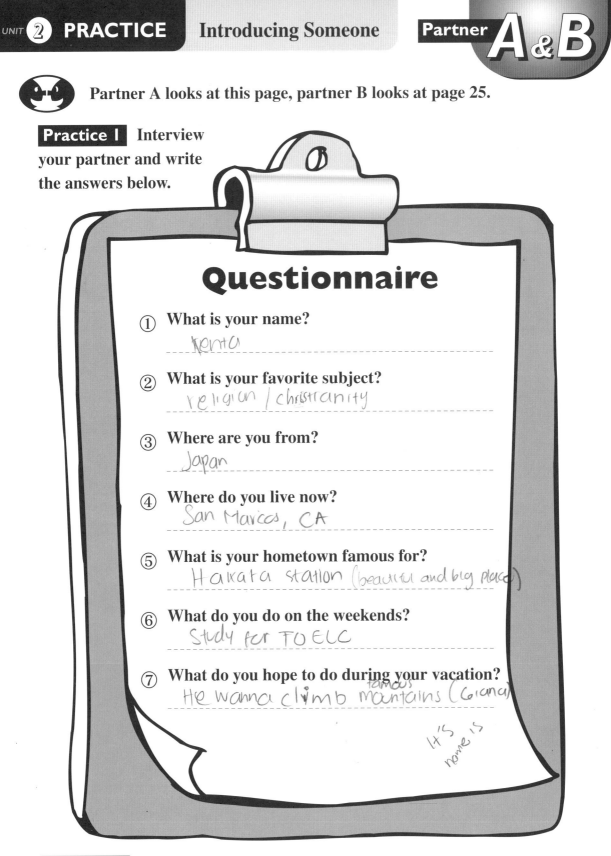

Questionnaire

① What is your name?

Kenta

② What is your favorite subject?

religion / christianity

③ Where are you from?

Japan

④ Where do you live now?

San Marcos, CA

⑤ What is your hometown famous for?

Hakata station (beautiful and big place)

⑥ What do you do on the weekends?

Study for TOEIC

⑦ What do you hope to do during your vacation?

He wanna climb famous mountains (Giana)

It's name is

Practice 2 Now, Partner B interviews Partner A. Partner A answers using the phrases on page 25.

Use the phrases below to answer your partner's questions.

① ...name?	● My name is ... ● I'm ... ● You can call me ...
② ...favorite subject?	● My favorite subject is... ● I'm good at ... ● I like studying ...
③ ...from?	● I'm originally from ... ● I grew up in ... ● I was raised in ...
④ ...live now?	● I live in ... ● I now live here in ... ● I still live there.
⑤ ...hometown famous for?	● My hometown is known for ... ● My hometown has a ... ● My hometown is famous for ...
⑥ ...on the weekend?	● On the weekends, I like ... ● On my days off, I always/usually/sometimes ... ● On Saturdays and Sundays, I always/usually/sometimes ...
⑦ ...during your vacation?	● I hope to ... during summer vacation. ● This summer, I want to ... ● During my next vacation, I would like to ...

Introducing Someone

Select from these phrases to introduce your partner to the class:

Person's Name:	**This is our teacher, • • •** **This is my friend, • • •** **This is our classmate, • • •**
Favorite Subject:	**He tells me his favorite subject is • • •** **He likes studying • • •** **His favorite subject is • • •**
Hometown:	**He is originally from • • •** **He was raised in • • •** **He grew up in • • •**
Residence:	**He now lives over in • • •** **He still lives there.** **He now lives here in • • •**
Hometown's Claim to Fame:	**He says • • • is known for • • •** **He says that • • • is famous for • • •** **He says that • • • has a • • •**
Weekends:	**On the weekends, he usually • • •** **On Saturdays and Sundays, he sometimes • • •** **On his days off, he always • • •**
Vacation Plans:	**He hopes to • • • during summer vacation.** **During his next vacation, he would like to • • •** **This summer, he wants to • • •**
Closing:	**Please give him a warm welcome.** **Let's welcome him.** **Let's give him a warm welcome.**

Name:
This is my friend, ...
This is our classmate, ...
Favorite Subject:
He tells me his favorite subject is ...
He likes studying ...
His favorite subject is ...
Hometown:
He is originally from ...
Vacation Plans:
He hopes to ... during summer vacation.
During his next vacation, he would like to ...
This summer, he wants to ...
Closing:
Please give him a warm welcome.
Let's welcome him.
Let's give him a warm welcome.
26
This is...
Getting Ready for SPEECH
Monday

Introduce your partner!

Step 1 CHOOSE

Choose a phrase from page 26 for each of the speaking points.

Step 2 WRITE

Write the phrase and add your partner's personal information from the questionnaire on page 24.

Step 3 SPEAK

Use this page to introduce your partner.

Speaking Points

Introduction
- Person's Name ______________________

Body
- Favorite Subject ______________________
- Hometown ______________________
- Residence ______________________
- Hometown's Claim to Fame ______________________
- Weekends ______________________
- Vacation Plans ______________________

Conclusion
- Closing ______________________

Exercise 1 Read the sentences and circle the best place to insert the adverb of frequency in parentheses. The first one is done for you.

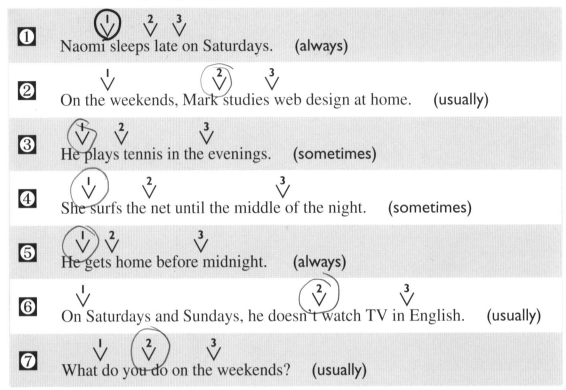

1. Naomi [1] sleeps [2] late [3] on Saturdays. (always)
2. On [1] the weekends, Mark [2] studies [3] web design at home. (usually)
3. He [1] plays [2] tennis in the [3] evenings. (sometimes)
4. She [1] surfs [2] the net until the middle [3] of the night. (sometimes)
5. He [1] gets [2] home before [3] midnight. (always)
6. On [1] Saturdays and Sundays, he doesn't [2] watch TV [3] in English. (usually)
7. What [1] do you [2] do on [3] the weekends? (usually)

Exercise 2 Read the sentences and circle the correct verb or pronoun. The first one is done for you.

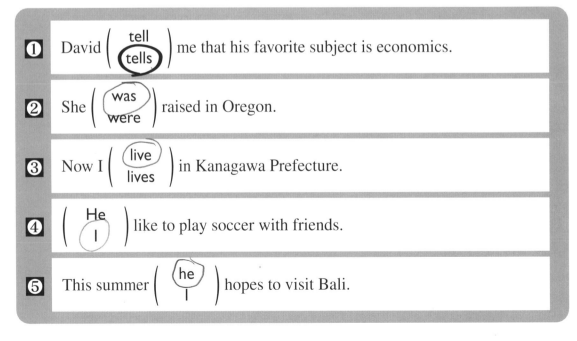

1. David (tell / tells) me that his favorite subject is economics.
2. She (was / were) raised in Oregon.
3. Now I (live / lives) in Kanagawa Prefecture.
4. (He / I) like to play soccer with friends.
5. This summer (he / I) hopes to visit Bali.

Getting Ready for Speech

~ Informative Speeches ~

Demonstration

ABOUT THIS UNIT

Goal	Learn how to demonstrate something to an audience
Key Language	First/Next/Then ~ Turn on/Plug into ~ Remember to ~
Delivery Focus	Gestures of sequence and demonstration
Final Speech	Do a demonstration speech in front of the class

Demonstration Speech

Listen to this demonstration speech. Number the pictures in the storyboard in the proper order.
The first one is done for you.

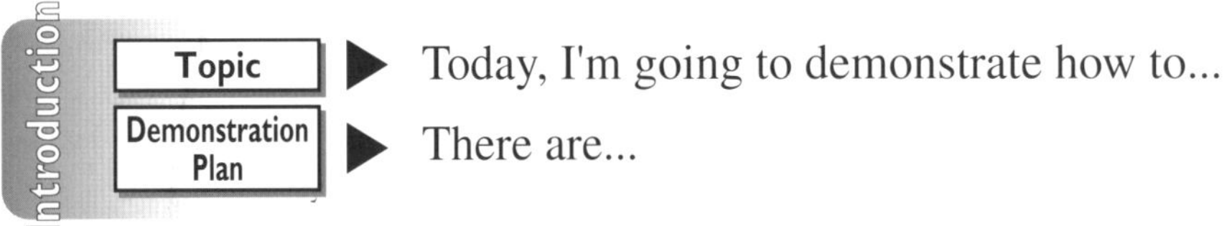

Topic ▶ Today, I'm going to demonstrate how to...

Demonstration Plan ▶ There are...

Story Board

Body

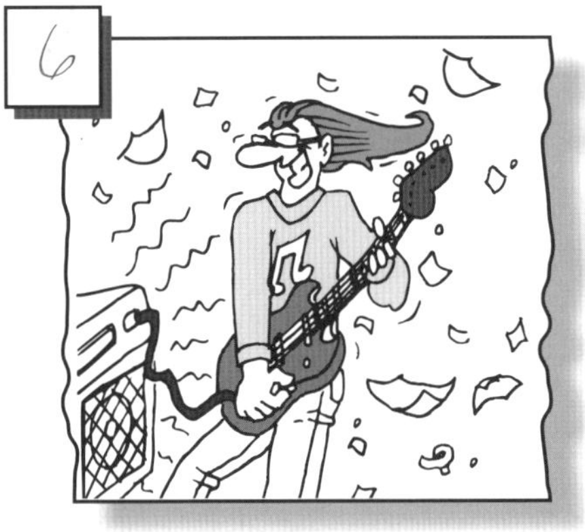

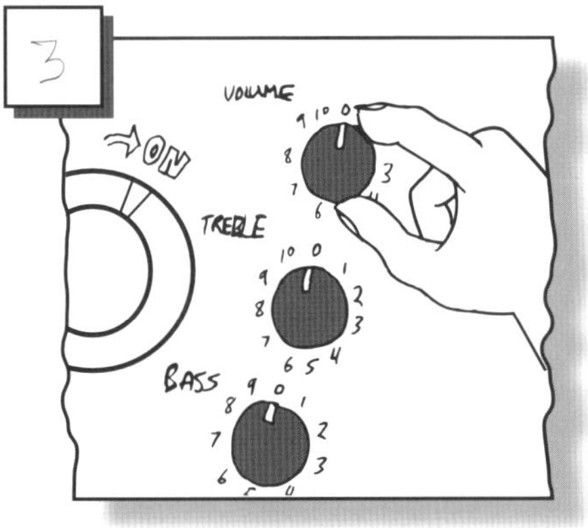

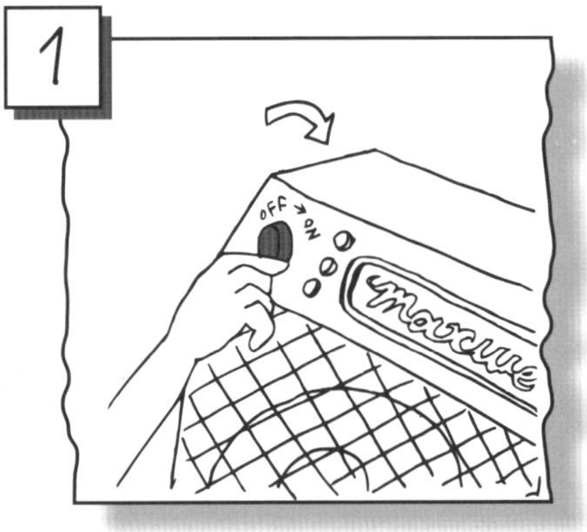

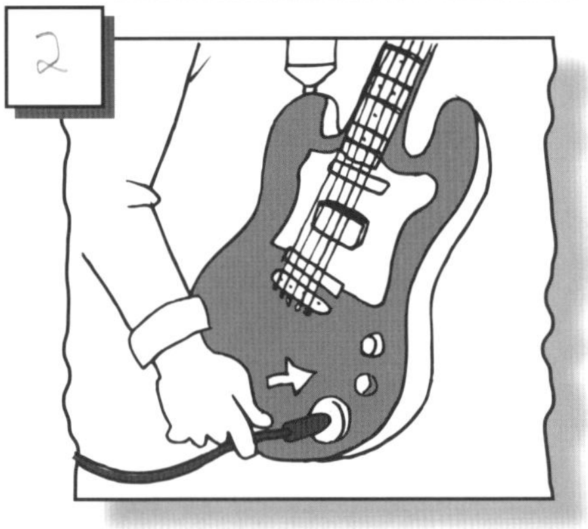

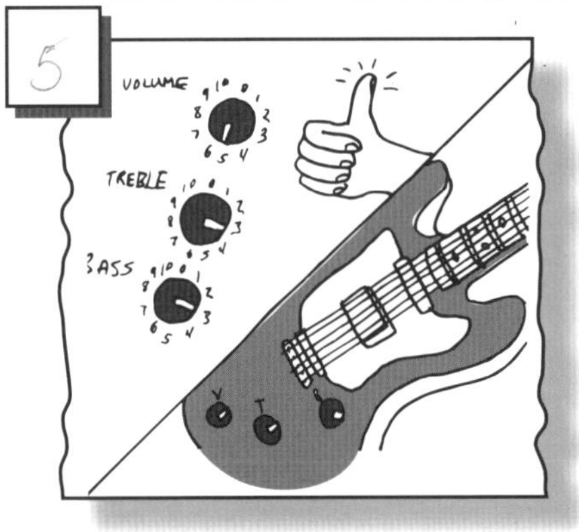

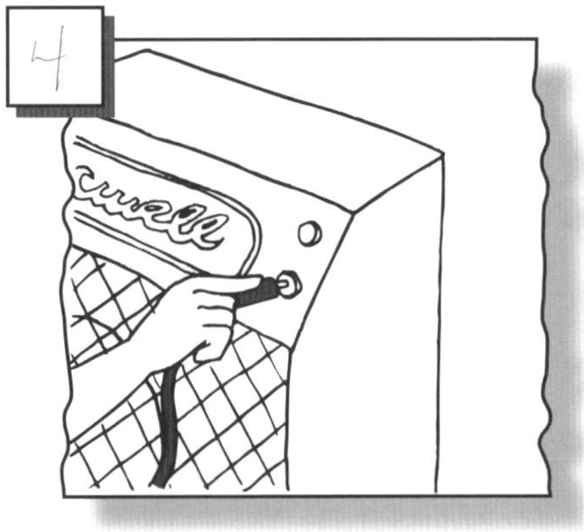

Closing ▶ That is how you connect your electric guitar to your amplifier! Thank you.

Listen to this demonstration speech. Number the pictures in the storyboard in the proper order.

Listening 2

Introduction

Topic ▶ Today, I'm going to show you...

Demonstration Plan ▶ There are...

Story Board

Body

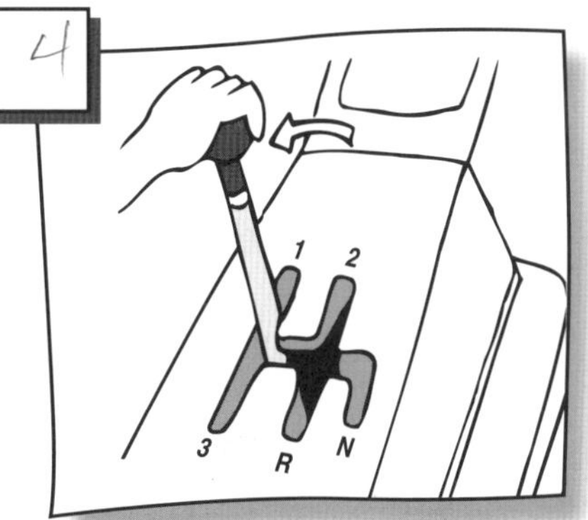

Conclusion

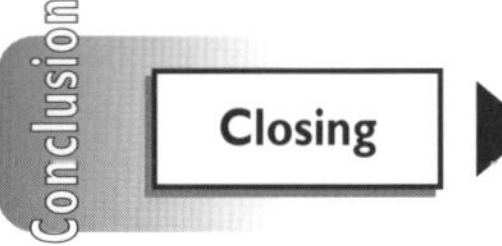

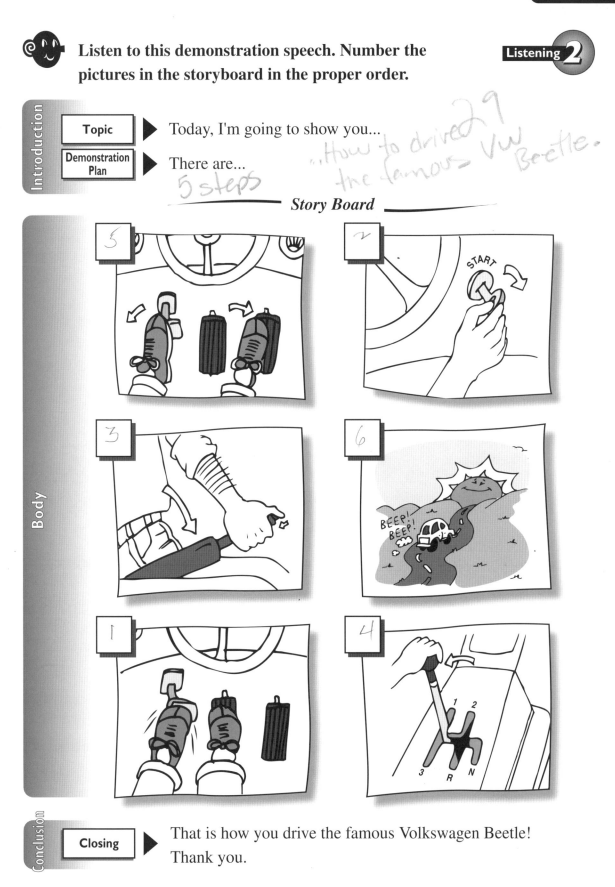

Closing ▶ That is how you drive the famous Volkswagen Beetle! Thank you.

Study these expressions for demonstration speeches.

Topic:	**I am going to demonstrate how to** connect your electric guitar to your amplifier. **I'm going to show you how to** drive the famous VW Beetle.
Demonstration Plan:	**There are** five **main steps.** **There are** five **steps.**
Sequencers:	**First, Next, Then, After that, Finally,** **First, Second, Third, Fourth, Fifth,** **The first step is to..., The second step is to...,** **In the first step..., In the second step...,**
Commands:	**turn on** your amplifier **plug the** other end of the guitar cord **into the** amplifier **adjust the** volume, treble and bass controls **on the** amp **push in the** clutch with your left foot **put the** key **in the** ignition **turn it to** the right **start the** car **release the** emergency brake **shift** into 1st gear **by** moving the gearshift to the upper left position **move** your right foot **from** the brake **to** the accelerator
Simultaneous Actions:	**While** waiting for your amplifier to warm up, **plug** the guitar cord into the bottom of the guitar. **Let out the** clutch with your left foot **while pushing down** on the accelerator with your right foot.
Warnings:	**Make sure that** the volume control is turned to zero. **Remember to** let the clutch out slowly.

Let's try! Listen and follow the instructions.

To watch a video

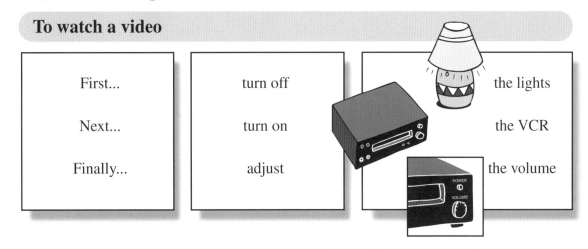

First...	turn off	the lights
Next...	turn on	the VCR
Finally...	adjust	the volume

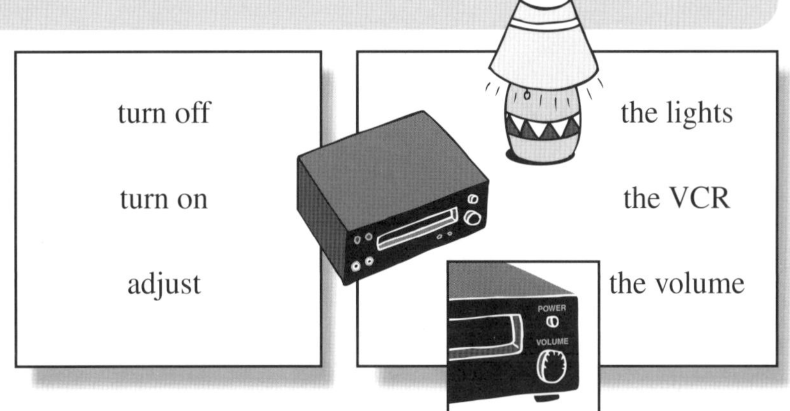

To call the police

First...	find	a pay phone
Second...	lift	the receiver
Third...	press	911

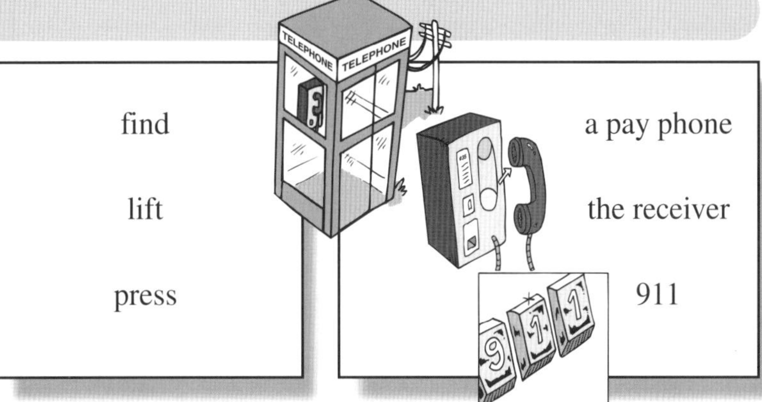

To make tea

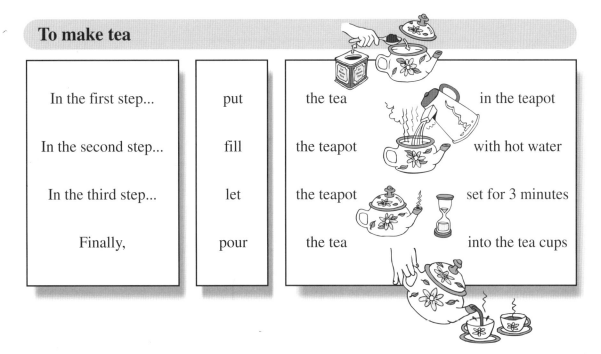

In the first step...	put	the tea	in the teapot
In the second step...	fill	the teapot	with hot water
In the third step...	let	the teapot	set for 3 minutes
Finally,	pour	the tea	into the tea cups

Gestures of Sequence

Practice these gestures of sequence:

First... | Second... | Third...

The first step... | The second step... | The third step...

First... | Next... | Finally...

Gestures of Demonstration

Practice these gestures of demonstration:

1 adjust the volume

2 turn it to the right

3 push the button

4 put the key in the ignition

5 release the emergency brake

6 open the top

7 close the top

8 pick up the box

9 place it on the table

Partner A looks at this page. Partner B looks at page 38.

Practice 1 **Read this demonstration speech to your partner. Use gestures!**

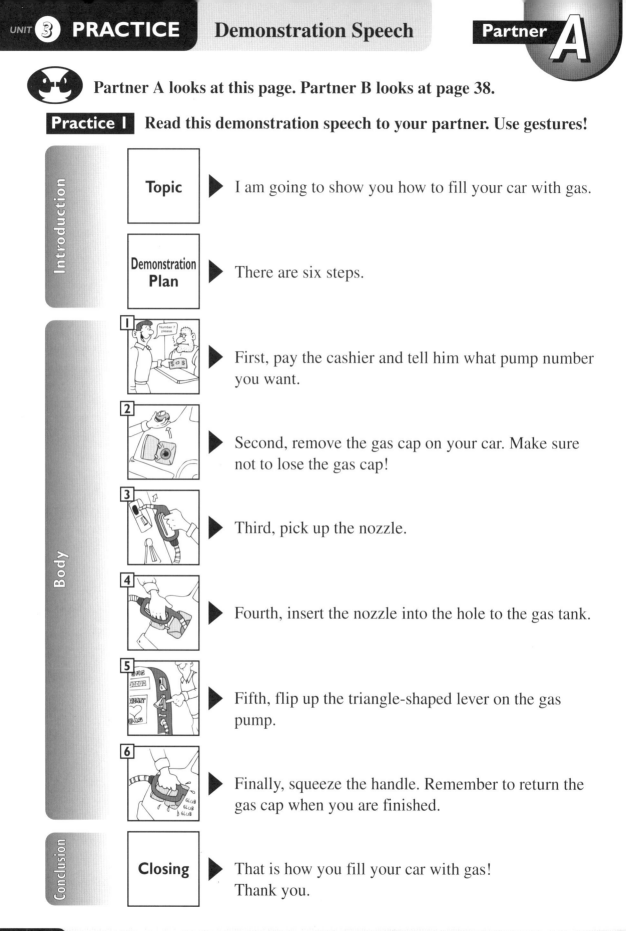

Introduction

Topic ▶ I am going to show you how to fill your car with gas.

Demonstration Plan ▶ There are six steps.

Body

1

▶ First, pay the cashier and tell him what pump number you want.

2

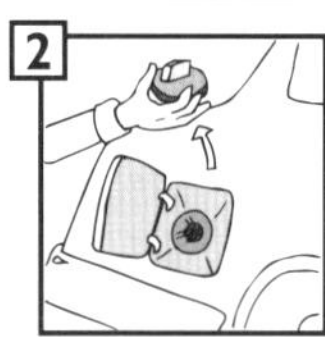

▶ Second, remove the gas cap on your car. Make sure not to lose the gas cap!

3

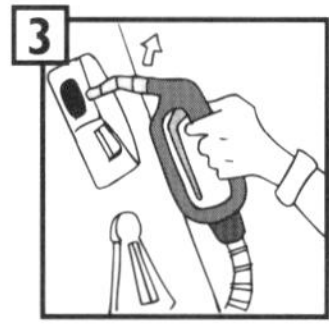

▶ Third, pick up the nozzle.

4

▶ Fourth, insert the nozzle into the hole to the gas tank.

5

▶ Fifth, flip up the triangle-shaped lever on the gas pump.

6

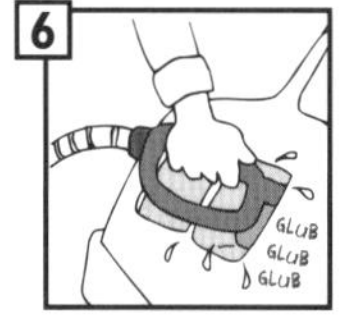

▶ Finally, squeeze the handle. Remember to return the gas cap when you are finished.

Conclusion

Closing ▶ That is how you fill your car with gas! Thank you.

Practice 2 **Listen to your partner read a demonstration speech. Number the pictures in the storyboard in the proper order.**

Introduction

Topic ▶	I am going to demonstrate how to wash your clothes at the laundromat.
Demonstration Plan ▶	There are six main steps.

Story Board

Body

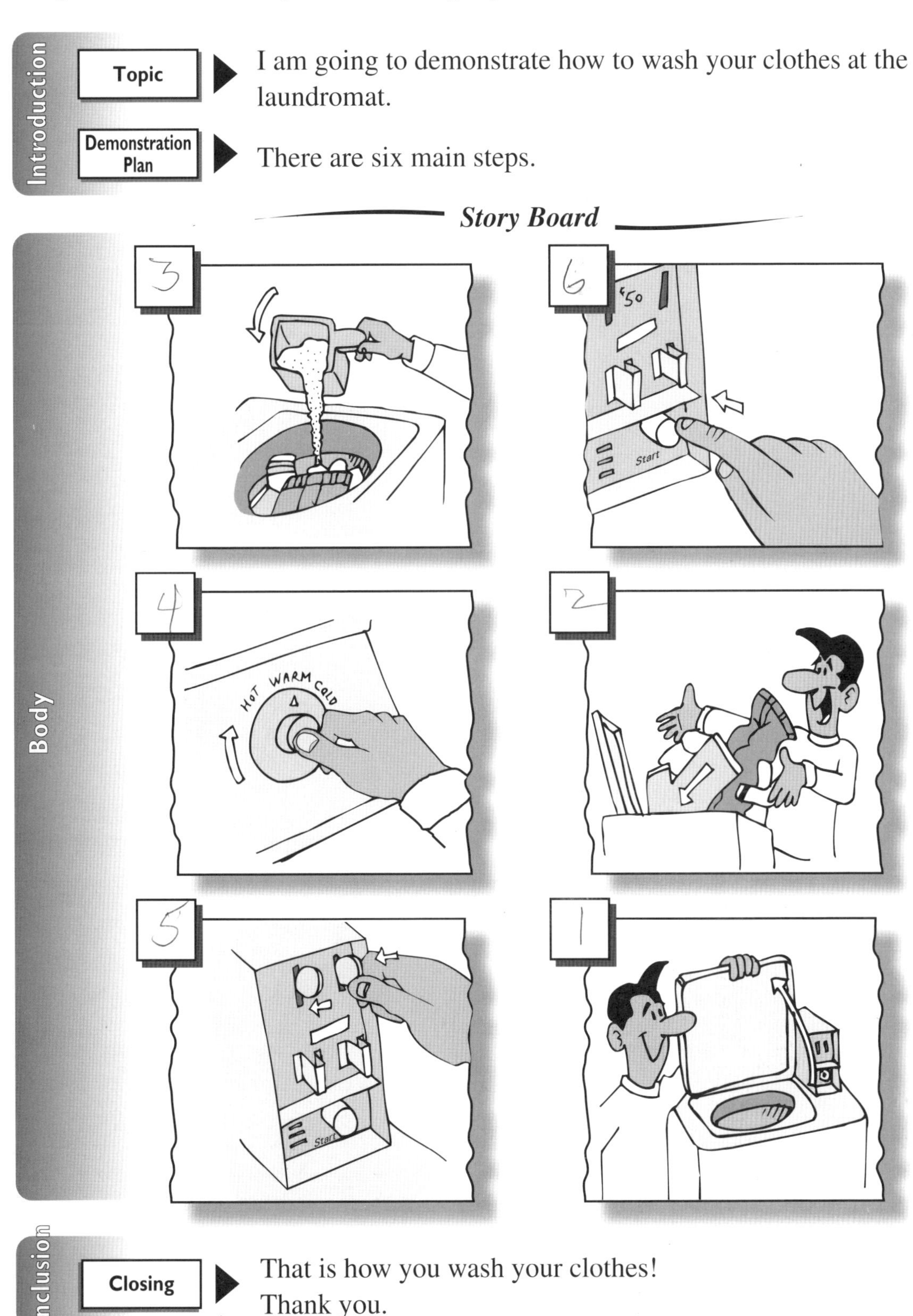

Conclusion

Closing ▶	That is how you wash your clothes! Thank you.

Demonstration Speech

Partner B

Practice I **Listen to your partner read a demonstration speech. Number the pictures in the storyboard in the proper order.**

Introduction

Topic	▶	I am going to show you how to fill your car with gas.
Demonstration Plan	▶	There are six steps.

Story Board

Body

6

GLUB GLUB GLUB

2

3

1

Number 7 please.

$ 0 $

5

GAS

20179

HEART

GAS

4

Conclusion

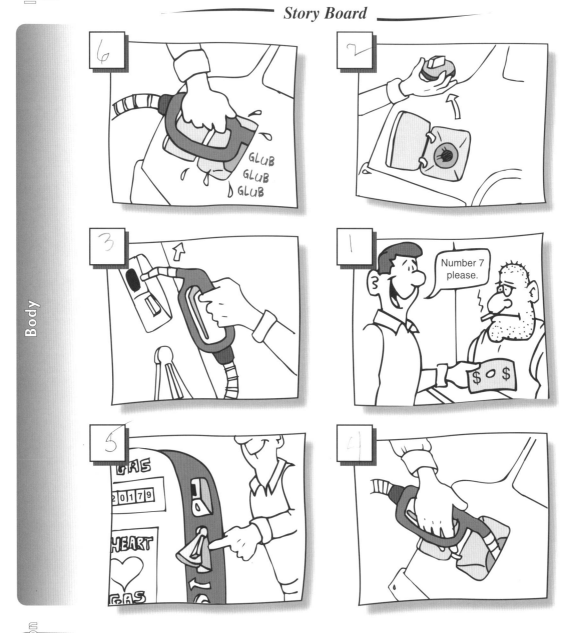

Closing	▶	That is how you fill your car with gas! Thank you.

Practice 2 **Partner B looks at this page. Partner A looks at page 37.**
Read this demonstration speech to your partner. Use gestures!

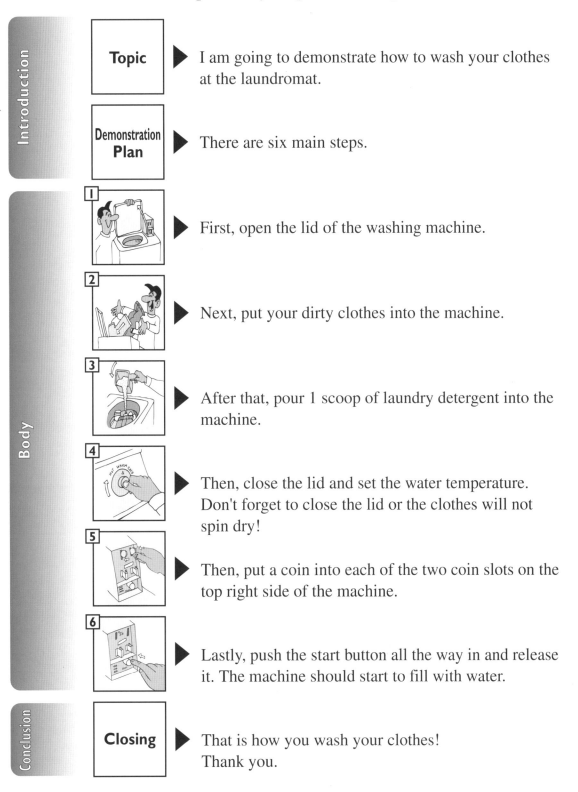

Introduction

Topic	I am going to demonstrate how to wash your clothes at the laundromat.
Demonstration Plan	There are six main steps.

Body

1	First, open the lid of the washing machine.
2	Next, put your dirty clothes into the machine.
3	After that, pour 1 scoop of laundry detergent into the machine.
4	Then, close the lid and set the water temperature. Don't forget to close the lid or the clothes will not spin dry!
5	Then, put a coin into each of the two coin slots on the top right side of the machine.
6	Lastly, push the start button all the way in and release it. The machine should start to fill with water.

Conclusion

Closing	That is how you wash your clothes! Thank you.

Demonstration Speech

Select from these phrases to make a demonstration speech:

Topic:	**I am going to demonstrate how to • • •** **I'm going to show you how to • • •**
Demonstration Plan:	**There are • • • main steps.** **There are • • • steps.**
Sequencers:	**First, Next, Then, After that, Finally,** **First, Second, Third, Fourth, Fifth,** **The first step is to • • • The second step is to • • •** **In the first step, • • • In the second step, • • •**
Commands:	**turn on • • •** **plug the • • • into the • • •** **adjust the • • • on the • • •** **push in the • • •** **put the • • • in the • • •** **turn it to • • •** **start the • • •** **release the • • •** **shift • • • by • • •** **move • • • from • • • to • • •**
Simultaneous Actions:	**While • • • , plug • • •** **Let out the • • • while pushing down • • •**
Warnings:	**Make sure that • • •** **Remember to • • •**

Make a storyboard for your demonstration speech! First, choose your demonstration topic. Then, select phrases from page 40 and draw pictures below. Finally, use this page to give your demonstration speech.

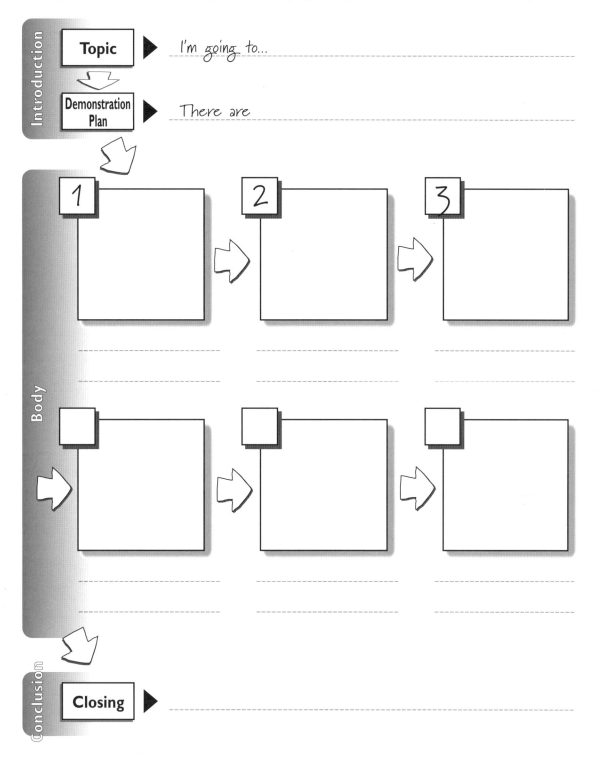

Introduction

Topic ▶ I'm going to...

Demonstration Plan ▶ There are

Body

1

2

3

Conclusion

Closing ▶

Exercise 1 **Complete the sentences by matching the beginning half of the sentence with the end. The first one has been done for you.**

① First, turn on C	A. the red button on the front.
② Next, press A	B. the temperature dial to 300 degrees.
③ Then, turn B	C. the oven.
④ Next, put E	D. the cake to cook, mix the frosting.
⑤ After that, let F	E. the cake in the oven.
⑥ While you are waiting for D	F. the cake cook for 30 minutes.
⑦ Then, take H	G. the frosting on the cake.
⑧ Finally, spread G	H. the cake out of the oven.

Exercise 2 **Put the following in the correct sequence.**

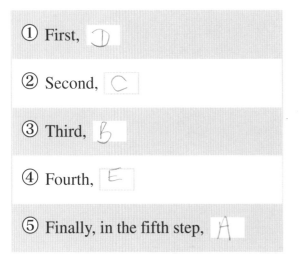

① First, D	A. Take out the can of soda.
② Second, C	B. Select the drink you want and press the button under the picture of the drink you chose.
③ Third, B	C. Put your money in the coin slot.
④ Fourth, E	D. Find a drink vending machine.
⑤ Finally, in the fifth step, A	E. Lift the small door at the bottom of the machine.

Getting Ready for Speech

~ Informative Speeches ~

Layout Speech

ABOUT THIS UNIT

Goal	**Learn how to explain layout, location, and position**
Key Language	**On the right ~ above/next to ~ in the northwest corner ~**
Delivery Focus	**Gestures of location and shape**
Final Speech	**Present the layout of your home to the class**

Listen and label the parts of the electronic drum kit. The first one is done for you.

Listening 1

Electronic Drum Set

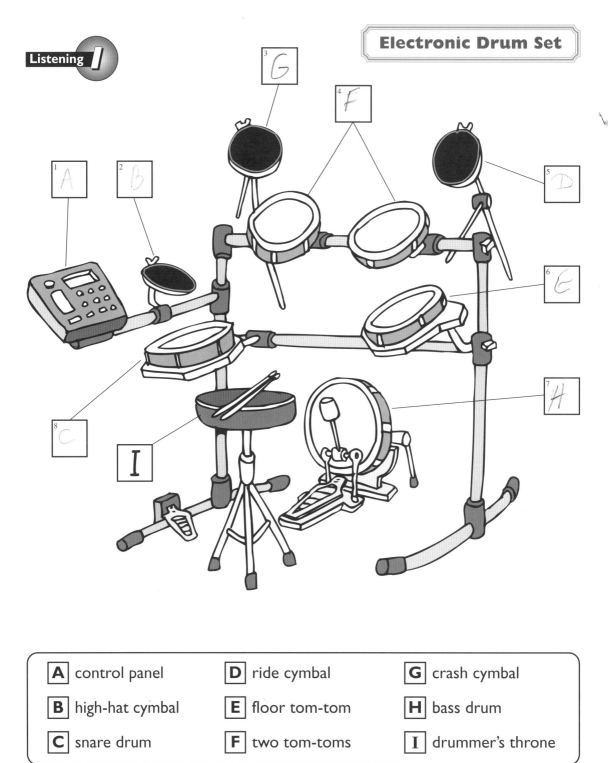

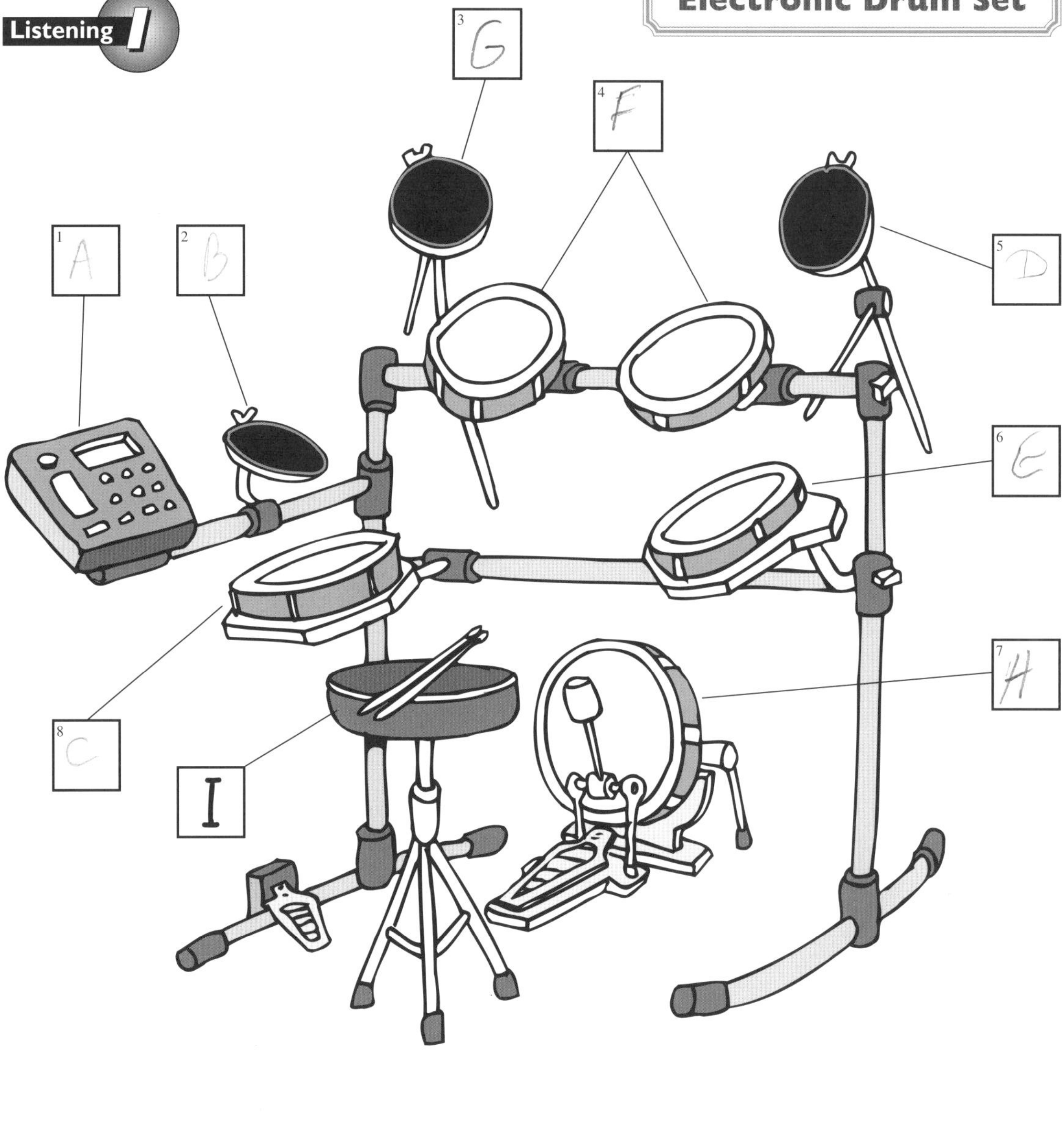

A control panel	**D** ride cymbal	**G** crash cymbal
B high-hat cymbal	**E** floor tom-tom	**H** bass drum
C snare drum	**F** two tom-toms	**I** drummer's throne

Listen and label the map of Sophia University.
The first one is done for you.

Listening 2

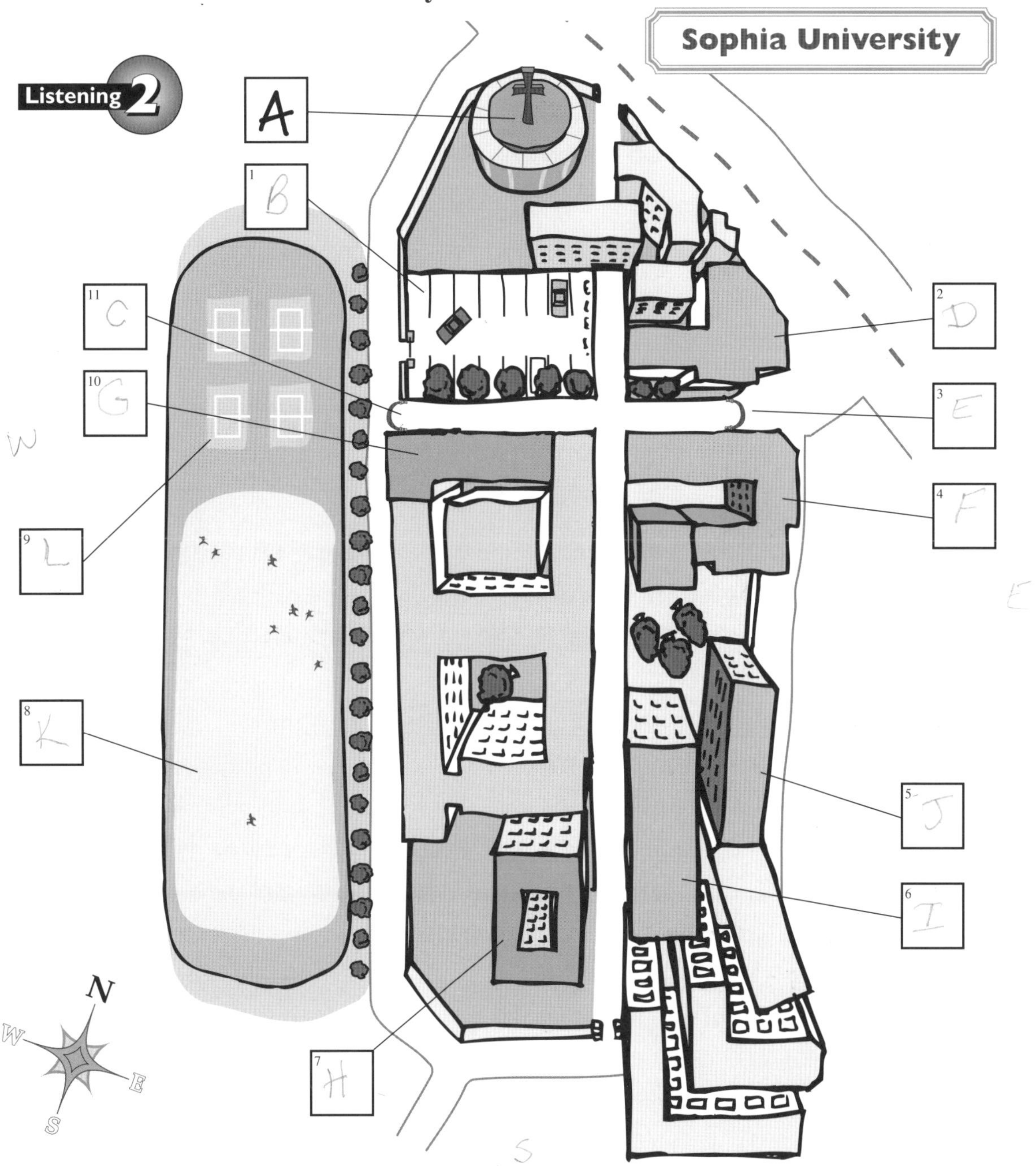

Sophia University

A — Saint Ignatius Church (example)

1 B
2 D
3 E
4 F
5 J
6 I
7 H
8 K
9 L
10 G
11 C

N / S / E / W

A	Saint Ignatius Church	**E**	East Gate	**I**	Central Library
B	parking lot	**F**	S.J. House	**J**	Krupp Hall
C	Main Gate	**G**	Building One	**K**	sports grounds
D	cafeteria & bookstore	**H**	computer center	**L**	tennis courts

Study these expressions for layout speeches.

Topic:	**I'd like to explain the layout of** your electronic drum kit. **I'd like to tell you about the layout of** the campus.
Layout:	The kit **is separated into** drums **and** cymbals. The campus **is divided into** four areas by two streets.
Explanation Plan:	**Beginning on the** left side **and moving to the** right... **Let's start on the** north side **and move** south.
Location by position:	The high-hat cymbal and pedal **are on the far left**. **Right in front of** you **is** the snare drum. The bass drum **is located in front of** your right foot. The bass drum **is beneath** the snare drum. **Above** the snare drum **are** two tom-toms. **On the left, above** the tom-toms, **is** the crash cymbal. **To the right of** that cymbal **is** the ride cymbal. The floor tom-tom **is located on the lower right side**. The cafeteria and bookstore **are next to** the east gate. **Across the street from** the computer center **is** the Central Library. **Behind** the library **is** Krupp Hall.
Location by compass points:	Saint Ignatius Church **is located in the northwest corner**. The parking lot **is located on the west side of** the campus. The cafeteria and bookstore **are to the east of** the parking lot. The Sophia sports grounds **are located along the west side**.
Shape:	**The square box** on the far-left side **is the** control panel. **The** horseshoe**-shaped** building **is the** S.J. House. **The** building **that looks like** a donut **is the** computer center.

  **Listen and follow the instructions.**

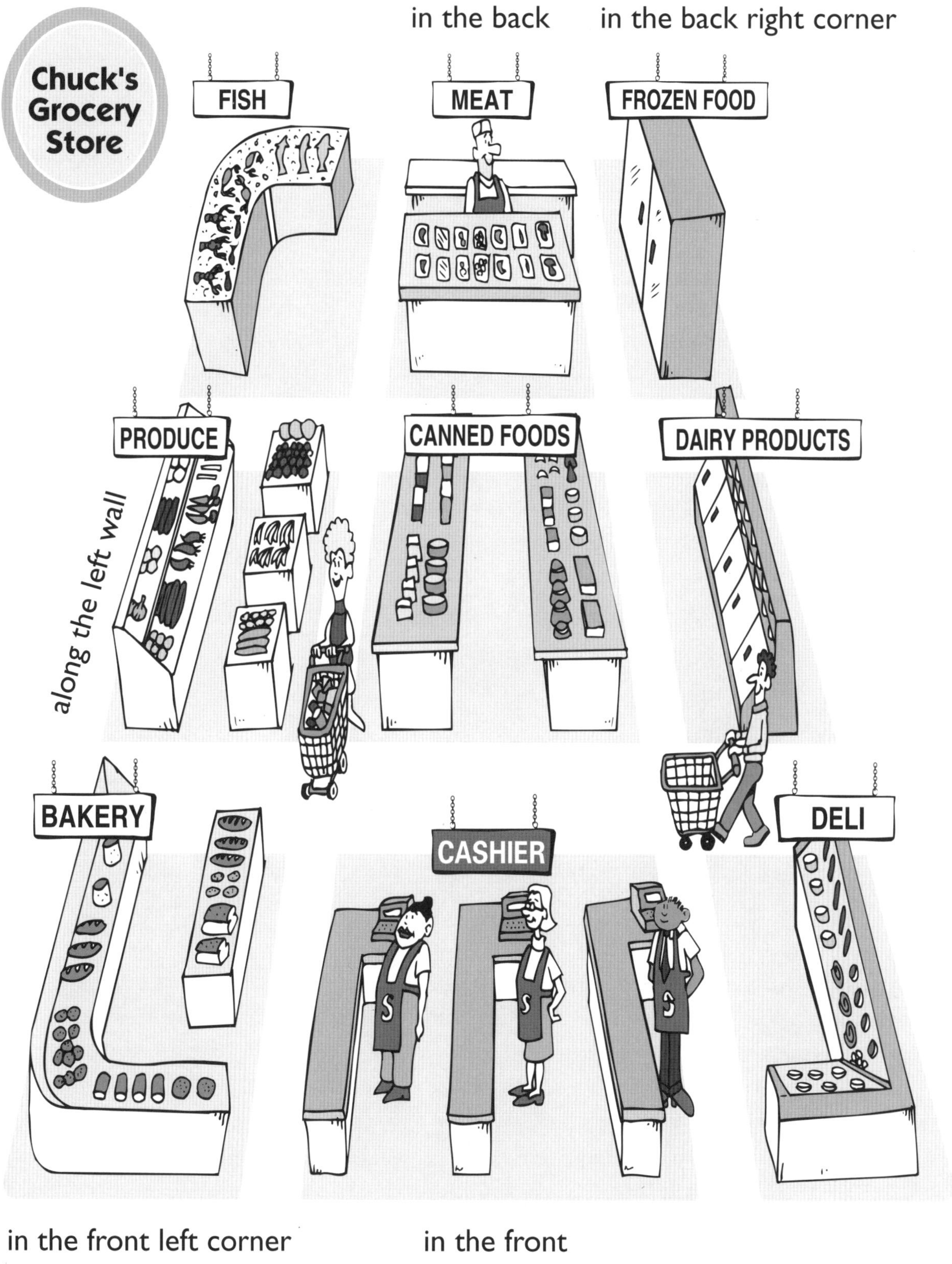

Gestures of Location

Practice these gestures of location:

1 In the northwest corner...

2 At the top of...

3 In the upper right corner...

4 To the left of...

5 In the middle of...

6 On the east side...

7 In the lower left hand corner...

8 Below.../beneath...

9 At the southern end...

Practice these gestures of shape:

The building is square.

It is a rectangular building.

The track is circular/round.

It is an oval track.

The pool is "S" shaped.

It is shaped like this.

Partner A looks at this page. Partner B looks at page 52.

Practice I **Read this layout speech of the Forbidden City in Beijing to your partner. Use gestures to help your partner understand the layout.**

■ I'd like to explain the layout of the Forbidden City, the ancient imperial palace of China. The Forbidden City is basically divided into 5 areas. Moving from south to north, they are the entrance gates, the outer court, the eastern exhibition halls, the inner court, and the imperial garden.

■ The road into the Forbidden City passes through four entrance gates. The largest of these gates is the outer gate, the Gate of Heavenly Peace. It faces Tiananmen Square and is sometimes used by important Chinese government officials for viewing parades.

■ The next area, the outer court, includes three huge meeting rooms or halls. The most famous of these is the Hall of Great Harmony. This hall was used only for special events or holidays such as New Year's. Nowadays, you can see the Great Imperial Throne there.

■ To the northeast of the outer court are the eastern exhibition halls. The most interesting of these is the Hall of Clocks. It is used for displaying the royal collection of clocks, watches, and timepieces. Most of the foreign timepieces came from Europe about 300 years ago in the 18th century.

■ Moving west, the next area is the inner court. The inner court was always off limits to everyone but the emperor and his family. Nowadays, of course, it is open to the public.

■ The final area, the Imperial Garden, is a huge park filled with many large, strangely shaped rocks. There are also many trees that are hundreds of years old. In this area, there are several kiosks selling refreshments and snacks.

■ Thank you for your attention.

Practice 2 **Listen to your partner read a layout speech of the White House. Label the drawing below. The first one is done for you.**

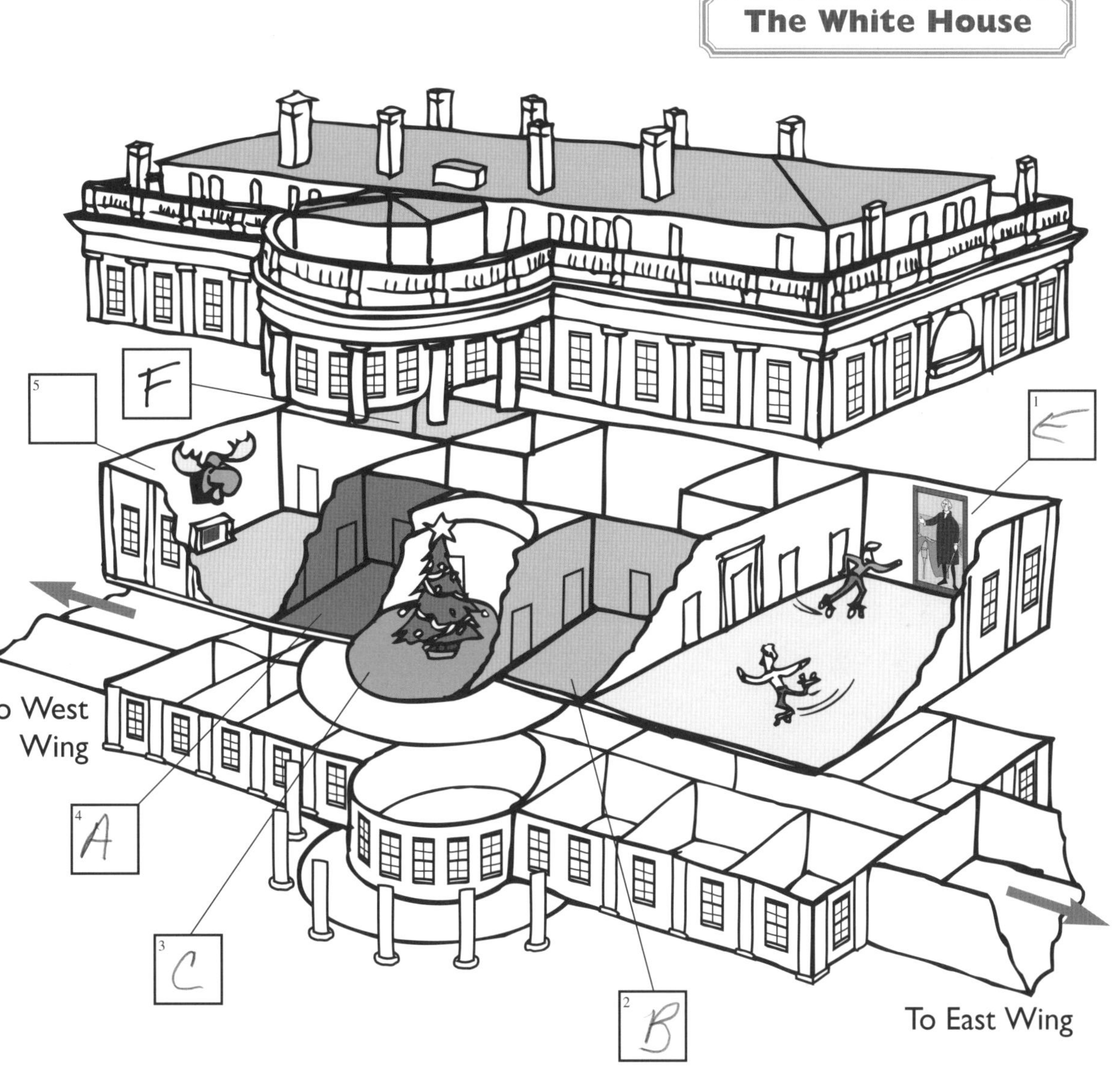

A	The Red Room	**D**	State Dining Room
B	The Green Room	**E**	The East Room
C	The Blue Room	**F**	The Family Dining Room

Partner B looks at this page. Partner A looks at page 50.

Practice 1 **Listen to your partner read a layout speech of the Forbidden City. Label the map below.**

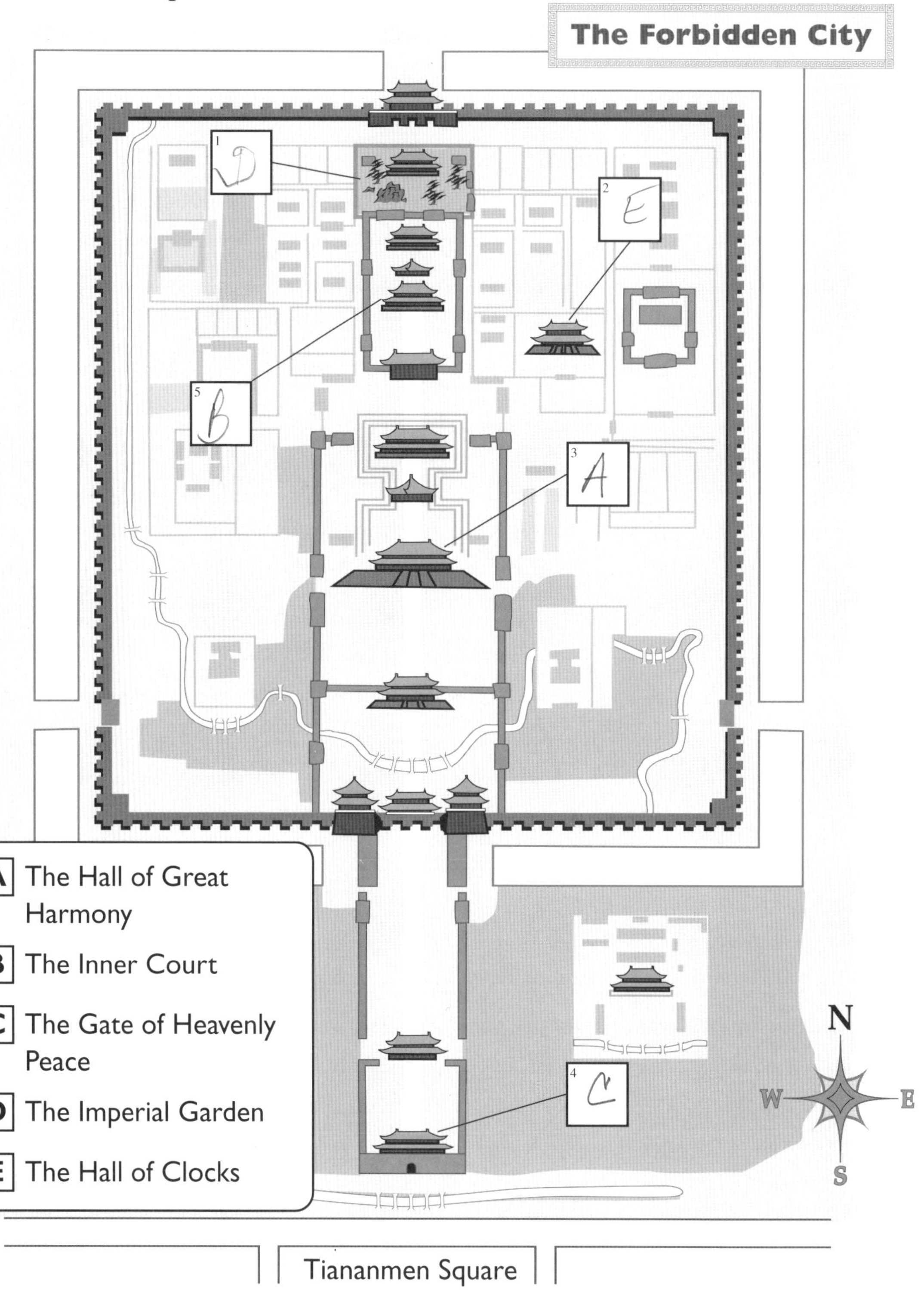

The Forbidden City

1 D
2 E
5 B
3 A
4 C

- **A** The Hall of Great Harmony
- **B** The Inner Court
- **C** The Gate of Heavenly Peace
- **D** The Imperial Garden
- **E** The Hall of Clocks

N W E S

Tiananmen Square

Practice 2 **Read this layout speech of the White House to your partner. Use gestures to help your partner understand the layout.**

1600 Pennsylvania Avenue, Washington, D.C.

● I'd like to tell you about the layout of the White House. The White House is basically divided into two areas: the areas open to the public, and the areas closed to the public. The areas open to the public are on the 2nd floor. The areas always off limits to the public include the first floor, the east and west wings, and the family dining room in the northwest corner, of the 2nd floor. Today's tour includes 5 rooms.

● Moving from east to west, the first room is the East Room. It is the largest room in the White House. It is sometimes used for large dances and receptions. The East Room is famous for the large full-length portrait of George Washington. This picture is the only object that has remained in the White House since 1800! In President Teddy Roosevelt's time his children sometimes used this large room for roller-skating.

● The second room is the Green Room. The president usually uses this room to greet foreign visitors. The newspapers and T.V. sometimes show the president speaking to famous guests in this room.

● The Blue Room is the oval shaped room. It is the most formal room in the White House. The White House Christmas Tree is always placed in this room. The oval shaped Blue Room should not be confused with the famous Oval Office, the president's private office located in the West Wing.

● To the west of the Blue room is the Red Room. It is the same size and shape as the Green Room and is sometimes used for small dinner parties.

● Finally, there is the State Dinning Room, the second largest room in the White House. It is used for large formal dinners and parties. It can seat 140 guests. In Teddy Roosevelt's day, a stuffed moose head hung above the fireplace.

● Thank you for your attention.

Layout Speech

Select from these phrases to make a speech explaining the layout of your home to the class:

Topic:	I'd like to explain the layout of ••• I'd like to tell you about the layout of •••
Layout:	••• is separated into ••• and ••• ••• is divided into •••
Explanation Plan:	Beginning on the ••• and moving to the ••• Let's start on the ••• and move •••
Location by position:	••• are on the far left. Right in front of ••• is ••• ••• is located in front of ••• ••• is beneath ••• Above ••• are ••• On the left, above •••, is ••• To the right of ••• is ••• ••• is located on the lower right side. ••• is next to ••• Across the street from ••• is ••• Behind ••• is •••
Location by compass points:	••• is located in the northwest corner. ••• is located on the west side of ••• ••• are to the east of ••• ••• are located along the west side.
Shape:	The square ••• is the ••• The ••• shaped ••• is the ••• The ••• that looks like a ••• is the •••

Present the layout of your home! Select phrases from page 54 and draw your home below. Then, use this page to give your layout speech.

Select phrases from page 54

Introduction

Topic ▶ I'd like to... my home.

Layout ▶ My home is...

Explanation Plan ▶

Body

Draw your home here

back

Nathan – Bedroom
Jason – Bedroom

front

Conclusion

Closing ▶

Look at the picture and fill in the blanks.

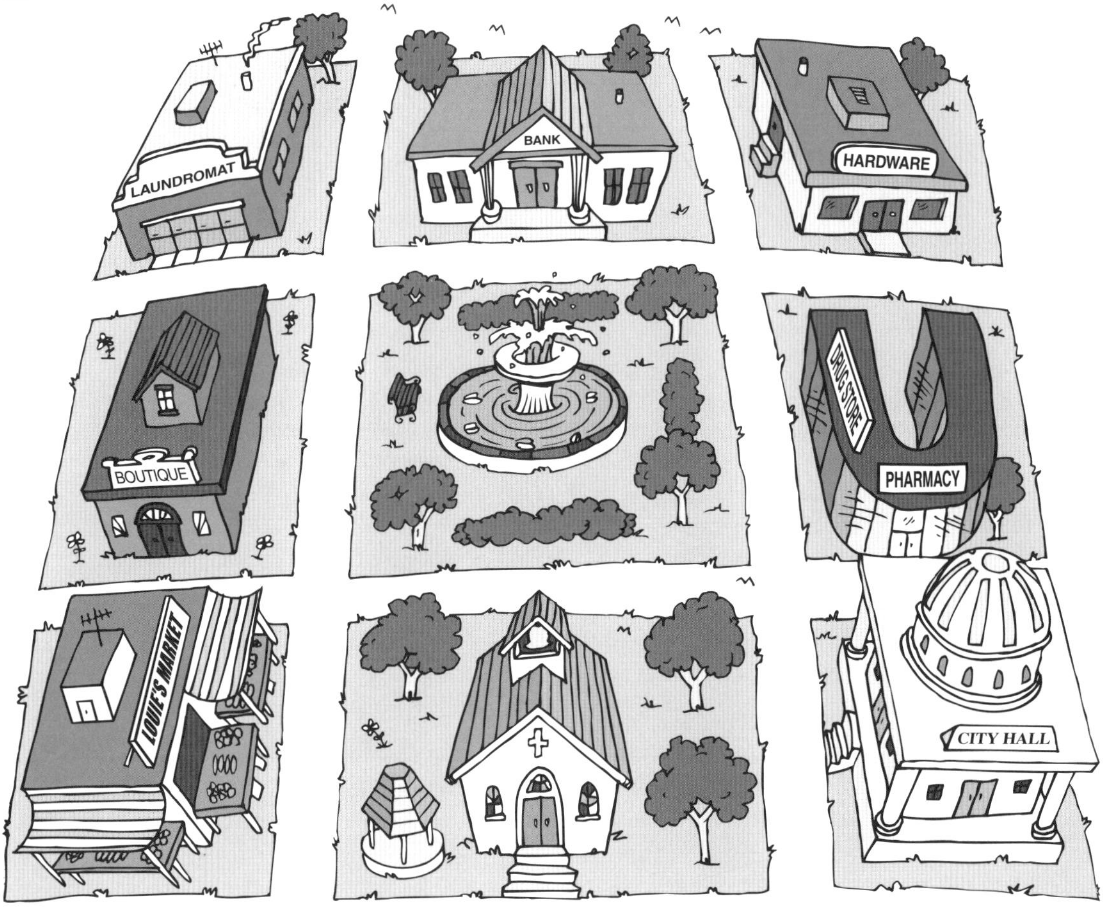

① Today, I'd like to tell you about the layout ______ my hometown.

② Right ______ ______ ______ you is the church.

③ The hardware store is located ______ the northeast corner.

④ The laundromat is ______ the upper left hand corner.

⑤ The boutique is ______ the left ______ the park.

⑥ The City Hall is ______ ______ the church.

⑦ The horse-shoe ______ building is the pharmacy.

⑧ Louie's Market is ______ the street ______ the church.

⑨ The church bell is ______ the top ______ the church.

⑩ The fountain is ______ the middle ______ the town.

Book and Movie Reviews

ABOUT THIS UNIT

Goal	Learn how to do oral reports
Key Language	Takes place before/during/after ~ In my opinion ~
Delivery Focus	Stressing important words for emphasis
Final Speech	Do a movie or book review in front of the class

Listen and complete the outline for the movie review.
Check (✔) the best ending for each point.

– Gone With The Wind –

I. About The Movie

A. *Gone with the Wind* is a classic movie

B. Won 10 Academy Awards

C. Takes place before, during, and after the American Civil War

II. The Story

A. Before the American Civil War

1. Rhett Butler meets beautiful
   - ❑ Scarlett O'Hara
   - ❑ Frankenstein
   - ❑ Ashley

2. Rhett falls in love with
   - ❑ Scarlett
   - ❑ Melanie
   - ❑ Scarlett's sister

3. Scarlett is in love with
- [x] Ashley
- [ ] Rhett
- [ ] Andrew

4. Ashley loves
- [x] Melanie
- [ ] Scarlett
- [ ] Rhett

B. During the war

1. Ashley goes off to
- [x] war
- [ ] school
- [ ] work

2. Melanie has a
- [x] baby
- [ ] job
- [ ] cow

3. Rhett rescues
- [ ] Scarlett
- [ ] Scarlett and Melanie
- [x] Scarlett, Melanie, and her baby

C. After the war

1. Scarlett marries
- [x] Rhett
- [ ] Ashley
- [ ] the General

2. they have
- [x] a child
- [ ] an argument
- [ ] a dog

3. the child
- [x] dies
- [ ] grows up
- [ ] leaves home

4. Rhett leaves
- [x] Scarlett
- [ ] work
- [ ] Melanie

III. My Opinion

A. Better than *Titanic*

B. Recommend that you watch this movie

Listen and complete the outline for the book review.
Check (✔) the best ending for each point.

Listening 2 – *The Little Prince* –

I. About The Book

A. *The Little Prince* went on sale in 1943

B. Over 50 million copies sold

1. more than 100 languages

II. The Story

A. The Little Prince's life on his home planet

1. the Little Prince lives alone
   - ☑ on a tiny planet the size of a house
   - ❑ on a desert island
   - ❑ in an enormous castle

a. there are no other children and
- ☑ no adults
- ❑ no animals and no flowers
- ❑ no other princes

b. his only friend is
- ☑ a small beautiful rose
- ❑ a wise little fox
- ❑ a giant yellow snake

2. one day, he decides to
- ☑ leave his planet
- ❑ leave the desert island
- ❑ leave the castle

B. The Little Prince's journey to earth

1. he visits
- ☑ 6 small planets and meets 6 adults
- ❑ 6 islands and plants 6 small roses
- ❑ 6 temples and meets 7 samurai

2. the Little Prince decides that
- ☑ adults are very strange
- ❑ roses are very beautiful
- ❑ samurai are very wise

C. The Little Prince's adventures on earth

1. he finds
- ☑ a wise fox
- ❑ some red rocks
- ❑ a guy's socks

2. the fox teaches him
- ☑ to see with his heart, not with his head
- ❑ to listen with his ears, not with his head
- ❑ to breathe through his nose, not his mouth

D. The Yellow Snake

1. a yellow snake helps him to
- ☑ return to his home planet
- ❑ return to his friend's house
- ❑ find his lost parents

III. My Opinion

(A). Simple words, not a simple message

B. Recommend that you read this book slowly and carefully

Book and Movie Reviews

Study these expressions for making book and movie reviews.

Topic:

I'd like to report on the classic movie, *Gone with the Wind.*
I'd like to summarize the popular book, *The Little Prince.*

Explanation Plan:

The movie can be divided into 3 **parts.**
This book can be divided into 4 **sections.**

Setting the Story:

Part 1 takes place before the American Civil War.
Part 2 takes place during the war.
Part 3 is after the war.
In the final scene, Scarlett suddenly realizes that she loves Rhett.
The first part describes the Little Prince's life on his home planet.
The second part of the book/movie/play covers covers the Little Prince's journey to Earth.
The third part of the book talks about his adventures on Earth.
In the final part, a yellow snake helps him to return to his home planet.

Storytelling Verbs:

Rhett Butler, **meets** Scarlett O'Hara.
Rhett **falls in love with** Scarlett
Ashley **goes off to** war
Melanie **has a baby**
Rhett **rescues** Scarlett and Melanie.
Scarlett **marries** Rhett
They **have a child**
The child **dies**
Scarlett **realizes that** she loves Rhett
Rhett **leaves** her

The Little Prince **lives** alone on a tiny planet.
One day, he **decides to leave** his planet
He **visits** 6 small planets
He **meets** 6 adults.
The Little Prince **decides that** adults are very strange.
He **finds** a wise fox.
The fox **teaches him to** see with his heart, not with his head.
A yellow snake **helps him to** return to his home planet.

Recommendation:

In my opinion, this is a much better drama than the 3 hour movie about a sinking ship.
I think that the words in this book are very simple, but the message is not.
I recommend reading this book slowly and carefully.

Let's try! Listen and follow the instructions.

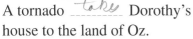

A tornado ________ Dorothy's house to the land of Oz.

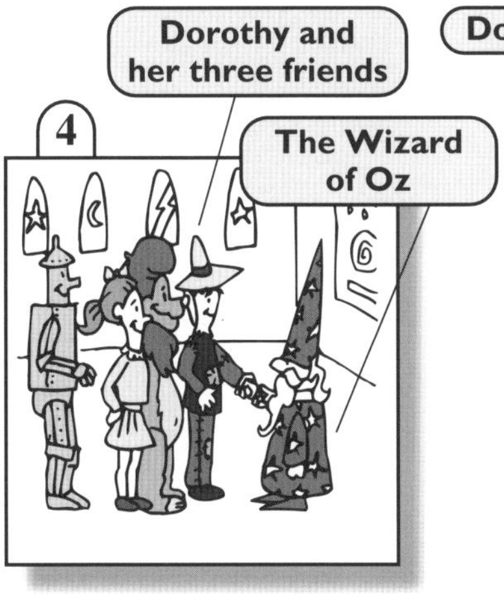

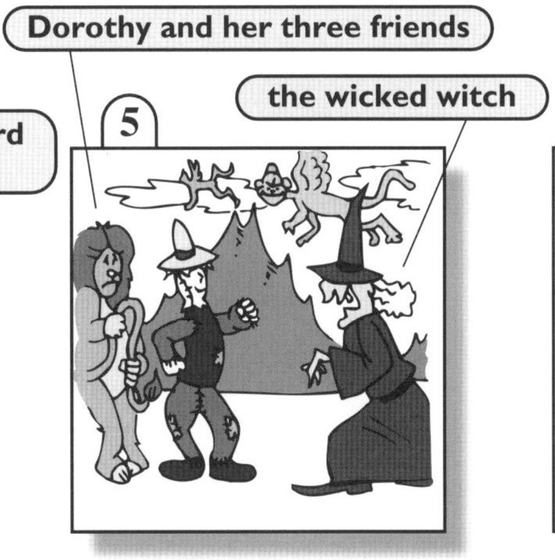

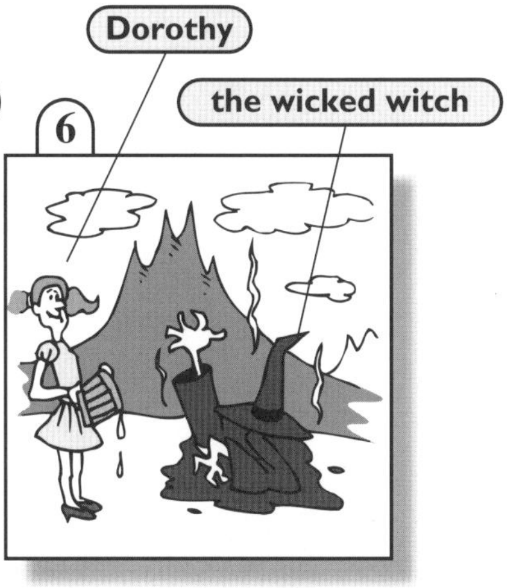

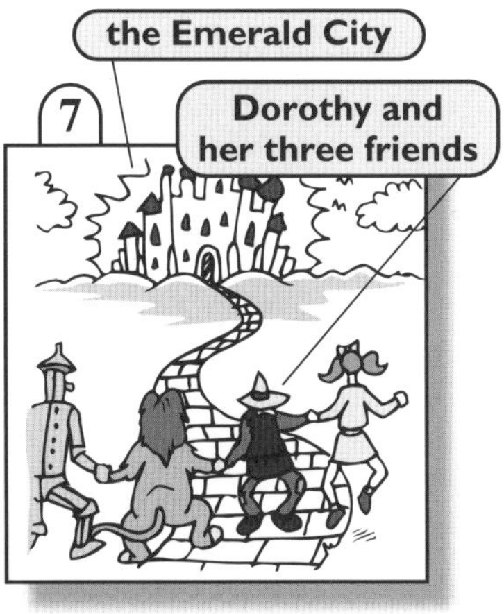

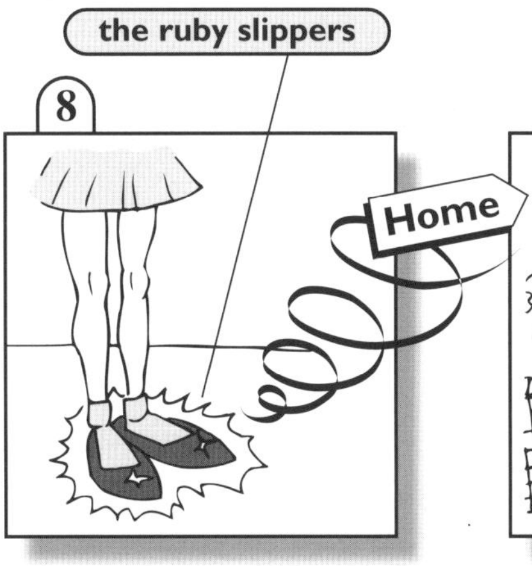

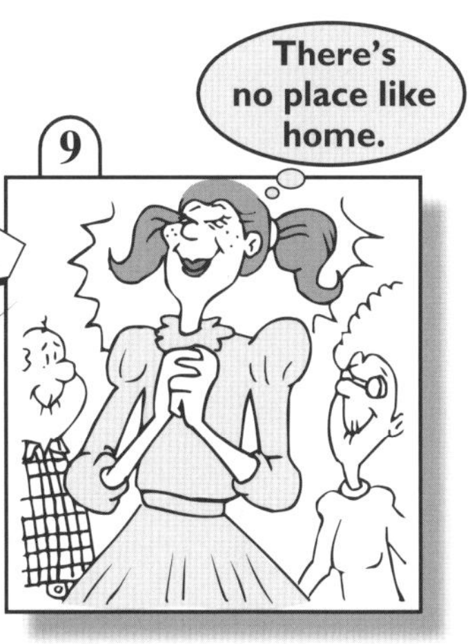

4
Dorothy and her three friends
The Wizard of Oz

5
Dorothy and her three friends
the wicked witch

6
Dorothy
the wicked witch

7
the Emerald City
Dorothy and her three friends

8
the ruby slippers
Home

9
There's no place like home.

Dorothy ________ "there's no place like home."

Listen to the following pairs of sentences.
Make a check next to the sentence that has emphasis.
The first one is done for you.

① ☐ **A:** I'd like to report on the classic movie *Gone with the Wind.*
☑ **B:** I'd like to report on the classic movie *Gone with the Wind.*

② ☐ **A:** In the first part of the movie, the hero, Rhett Butler, meets beautiful Scarlett O'Hara.
☐ **B:** In the first part of the movie, the hero, Rhett Butler, meets beautiful Scarlett O'Hara.

③ ☐ **A:** There are no other children and no adults.
☐ **B:** There are no other children and no adults.

④ ☐ **A:** The fox teaches him to see with his heart, not with his head.
☐ **B:** The fox teaches him to see with his heart, not with his head.

Listen to the following sentences and circle the numbers above the words that are emphasized.
The first one is done for you.

① (1) 2 3 4 (5) 6
In the first part of the movie, the hero, Rhett Butler, meets beautiful Scarlett O'Hara.

② 1 2 3 4 5 6 7
Rhett falls in love with Scarlett, but Scarlett is in love with Ashley and
8 9 10
Ashley is in love with Melanie.

③ 1 2 3 4 5 6 7 8
She and Rhett have a child but the child dies in an awful horseback riding
9
accident.

④ 1 2 3 4 5 6 7 8
The Little Prince lives alone on a tiny planet the size of a house.

⑤ 1 2 3 4 5 6 7 8
The Little Prince decides that adults are very strange and do not understand
9
life at all.

⑥ 1 2 3 4 5 6 7
I think that the words in this book are very simple, but the message is not.

 **Listen and repeat with emphasis.**

I do not recommend this book.

(2)

He falls madly in love with Hiromi.

(3)

Jack doesn't like Japan and he doesn't like Japanese baseball.

(4)

This is the fastest selling book in history.

(5)

In the final event...

(6)

In the first part of the movie...

(7)

You must read the book!

(8)

The Dragons beat the Giants.

Partner A looks at this page. Partner B looks at page 68.

Practice I **This is a book review.**
First, underline the words that you want to emphasize.
Read the review to your partner. Be sure to emphasize the key words.

I. About The Book

I'd like to report on the book, *Harry Potter and the Goblet of Fire.* This is the fastest selling book in history. It went on sale midnight July 8, 2000 and immediately sold 1.8 million copies. *Harry Potter and the Goblet of Fire* is a fantasy.

II. The Story

Harry is a young boy studying to be a wizard. Someone enters him in a dangerous contest with three older wizards. The 4 wizards compete in 3 events. In the first event, each wizard has to steal a golden egg guarded by a dragon. In the second event, the four wizards must swim to the bottom of a lake to rescue their best friends. In the final event, the four wizards must race each other to the center of a maze to find the Contest Cup. Who wins the contest? You must read the book!

III. My Opinion

In conclusion, this is a very exciting book. But I don't recommend it because it is over 600 pages long!!!

Practice 2 **Listen to Partner B and check the best ending for each point.**

– MR. BASEBALL OUTLINE –

I. About The Movie

A. *Mr. Baseball* is a
- ❏ funny movie
- ❏ serious movie
- ❏ cartoon

B. Jack Elliot is a Major League
- ❏ coach
- ❏ baseball player
- ❏ owner

C. He comes to Japan
- ❏ for a vacation
- ❏ to play baseball
- ❏ to make a movie

II. The Story

A. Jack doesn't like
- ❏ basketball
- ❏ baseball
- ❏ Japan and doesn't like Japanese baseball

1. Jack falls in love with the daughter of
   - ❏ the owner of the Chunichi Dragons
   - ❏ the manager of the Chunichi Dragons
   - ❏ the owner of the Seattle Mariners

2. Jack's batting
   - ❏ improves
   - ❏ is excellent
   - ❏ goes into a slump

B. Jack asks for help

1. Coach Uchiyama helps Jack
   - ❏ improve his pitching
   - ❏ improve his fielding
   - ❏ improve his batting

2. the Dragons
   - ❏ play the Giants
   - ❏ beat the Giants
   - ❏ tie the Giants

III. My Opinion

A. This movie is
- ❏ a shock
- ❏ about culture shock
- ❏ about how to beat the Giants

Practice I **Partner B looks at this page. Partner A looks at page 66. Listen to Partner A and check(✓)the best ending for each point.**

– *Harry Potter and the Goblet of Fire outline* –

I. About The Book

A. *Harry Potter and the Goblet of Fire* went on sale
- ❏ July 18, 2000
- ❏ June 18, 2001
- ❏ July 8, 2000

B. The book is
- ❏ a fantasy
- ❏ fantastic
- ❏ famous

II. The Story

A. Harry is in a contest with
- ❏ three other people
- ❏ three other dragons
- ❏ three other wizards

B. The first event

1. each wizard must steal
- ❏ a golden head
- ❏ a golden dragon
- ❏ a golden egg

C. The second event

1. each wizard rescues
- ❏ a young dragon
- ❏ their best friend
- ❏ a golden egg

D. The third event

1. a race to get
- ❏ the Contest Cup
- ❏ a trip to Hawaii
- ❏ the Wizard's Cup

III. My Opinion

A. This book is
- ❏ not exciting
- ❏ very long
- ❏ over 1600 pages

Practice 2 **This is a movie review.**
First, underline the words that you want to emphasize.
Read the review to your partner. Be sure to emphasize the key words.

I. About The Movie

I'd like to summarize the movie, *Mr. Baseball*. It is a funny movie about a major league baseball player, Jack Elliot. He comes to Japan to play baseball for the Chunichi Dragons. The movie can be divided into two parts.

II. The Story

In the first part of the movie, Jack doesn't like Japan and he doesn't like Japanese baseball. But he falls in love with Hiromi Uchiyama, the daughter of the manager of the Dragons. Jack's batting also falls into a slump. In the second part of the movie, Jack asks Coach Uchiyama to help him improve his batting. Coach Uchiyama gives him a very tough work out every morning. Soon, Elliot's batting improves and he becomes a good member of the Chunichi Dragons. In the final scene, the Dragons beat the Giants.

III. My Opinion

In conclusion, this movie is a story about culture shock. Jack learns that playing baseball in Japan is not the same as playing baseball in the US. I recommend this movie because it is very funny.

Select from these phrases to make a movie or book review:

Topic:	I'd like to report on • • • I'd like to summarize • • •
Explanation Plan:	The book/movie/play/story can be divided into • • • parts. This book/movie/play/story can be divided into • • • sections.
Setting the Story:	Part 1 takes place before/during/after • • • Part 2 takes place in/on/around • • • Part 3 is • • • The first part describes • • • The second part of the book/movie/play covers • • • The third part of the book talks about • • • In the final part, • • • In the final scene, • • •
Storytelling Verbs:	• • • meets • • • • • • falls in love with • • • • • • goes off to • • • • • • has a baby • • • rescues • • • • • • marries • • • • • • have a child • • • dies • • • realizes that • • • • • • leaves • • • • • • lives • • • • • • decides to leave • • • • • • visits • • • • • • meets • • • • • • decides that • • • • • • finds • • • • • • teaches him to • • • • • • helps him to • • •
Recommendation:	In my opinion • • • I think that • • • I recommend • • •

Make an outline for your book or movie review! First, choose a book or movie. Then, complete the outline below. Finally, use the phrases on page 70 and this outline to give your review.

Introduction

I. About The Book Or Movie

A. ____________________

1. ____________________

____

Body

II. The Story

A. ____________________

____

____

____

____

____

____

____

____

____

____

____

____

Conclusion

III. My Opinion

A. ____________________

The sentences below are missing some words. Choose the best words from the Word Box and write them in the blank spaces.

Word Box

sees win gets robs returns learns saves survive travels

① In the first scene, Rhett meets Scarlett at a party . He sees her there for the first time.

② The Little Prince leaves his home planet. He travels to six small planets.

③ In the last part of the movie, Dorothy goes back home. She returns to her house in Kansas.

④ In the final scene, Jack dies in the icy North Atlantic waters. He doesn't survive the sinking of the Titanic.

⑤ The wise fox teaches the Little Prince an important lesson. He learns how to see with his heart, not his head.

⑥ In the movie, the firefighter rescues the little boy from the burning house. He saves him from the fire.

⑦ The wizard steals the egg from the dragon. He robs the dragon of the egg.

⑧ Elliot's batting improves. His batting gets better.

⑨ The Dragons beat the Giants. The Dragons win the game!

Getting Ready for Speech

~ Storytelling ~

Show and Tell

ABOUT THIS UNIT

Goal	Learn how to present data to an audience
Key Language	It is 333 meters high ~ It was finished in ~
Delivery Focus	Pausing to emphasize important words
Final Speech	Explain a photograph, postcard or similar object to the audience

Listen and complete the Fact File below:

Listening 1

Fact File

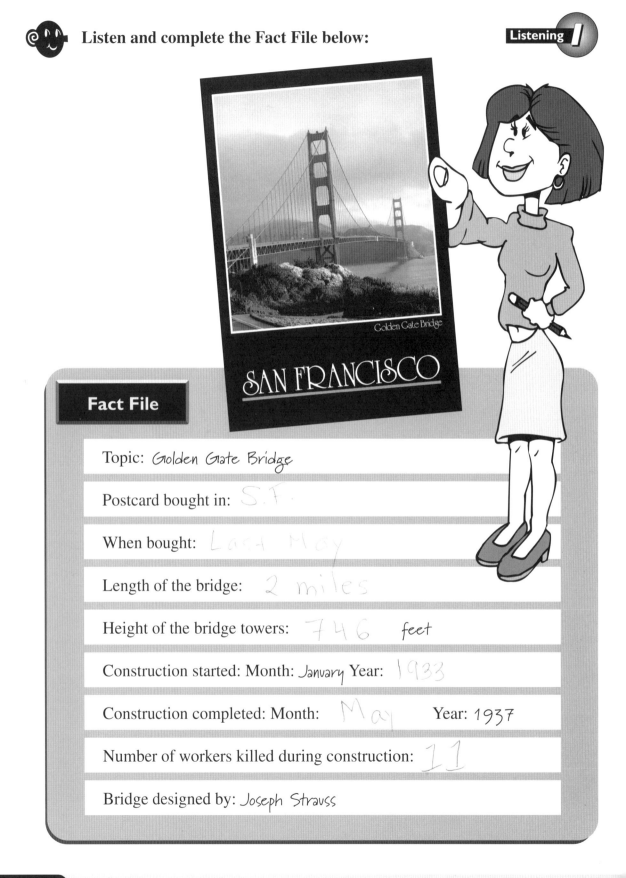

Topic: Golden Gate Bridge

Postcard bought in: S.F.

When bought: Last May

Length of the bridge: 2 miles

Height of the bridge towers: 746 feet

Construction started: Month: January Year: 1933

Construction completed: Month: May Year: 1937

Number of workers killed during construction: 11

Bridge designed by: Joseph Strauss

Listen and complete the Fact File below:

Fact File

Topic: Crater Lake

Photo taken by: father

When taken: 6 years ago.

Name of deepest lake in the U.S.: Crater Lake

Depth of Lake: 1932 feet

Distance across: 6 miles

Lake formed by: Volcanic Explosion

When formed: over 7000 years ago.

Study these expressions for show and tell.

Topic:

This is a postcard of the Golden Gate Bridge.
This is a photograph of me at Crater Lake National Park.

Tell your Story:

I bought it in San Francisco last May.
The weather in San Francisco was great!
The sun shone every day.
We rented bicycles and rode across the bridge.

It was taken by my father about 6 years ago.
We camped out and slept in a tent.
One night we heard a big bear in our camp site.
We were very quiet and finally it left.

Tell its Story:

Present:

The bridge is almost two miles long.
The towers are 746 feet tall.
Crater Lake is the deepest lake in the United States.
It is 1,932 feet deep.
It is about 6 miles across.

Past:

The Golden Gate Bridge was built during the Great Depression.
It was started in January 1933.
It was completed in May 1937.
Over 160,000 miles of wire cable were used to construct the bridge.
Eleven workers were killed during the construction of the bridge.
The bridge was designed by chief engineer, Joseph Strauss.
Over 400 bridges were built by him all over the world.
The lake was formed over 7,000 years ago when a volcano exploded.
This explosion was heard, and reported, by the Native Americans in the area.
Over 5000 square miles were covered with 6 inches of ash.

Closing:

In conclusion, the Golden Gate Bridge was a great engineering success. Today, it is a majestic landmark of San Francisco.
In conclusion, Crater Lake shows us the beauty of nature and its incredible power.

Let's try!  **Listen and follow the instructions.**

Fact File 1

Tokyo Tower

1. Height: 776 feet
2. Weight: 4,000 tons
3. Finished: 1958
4. Paint used: 28,000 liters

Fact File 2

Petronas Twin Towers

1. Height: 451.9 meters
2. Cost: US$1.2 billion
3. Started: 1993
4. Finished: 1996

Fact File 3

Starry Night

1. Painted by: Vincent van Gogh
2. Painted in: 1889
3. Displayed in: The Museum of Modern Art in New York
4. Date Acquired: 1941

UNIT 6 DELIVERY Emphasis II

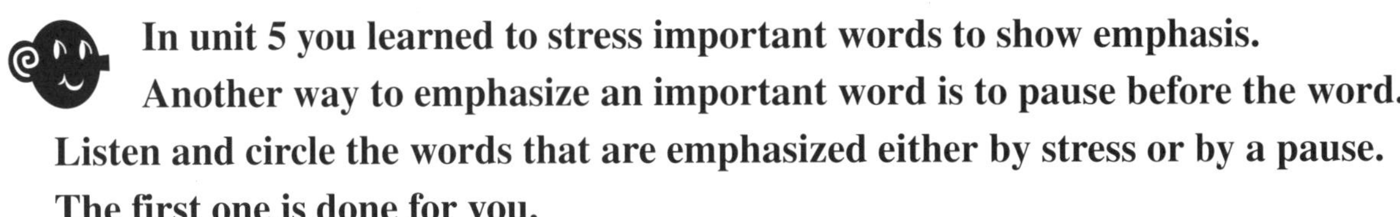

In unit 5 you learned to stress important words to show emphasis. Another way to emphasize an important word is to pause before the word. Listen and circle the words that are emphasized either by stress or by a pause. The first one is done for you.

① The weather in San Francisco was great!

② The sun shone every day.

③ The bridge is almost two miles long and the towers are 746 feet tall.

④ Over one hundred sixty thousand miles of wire cable were used to construct the bridge.

⑤ Over four hundred bridges were built by him all over the world.

⑥ In conclusion, the Golden Gate Bridge was a great engineering success.

Find the pause. Circle the number where you hear the pause. The first one is done for you.

① The sun (1) shone (2) every day.

② The bridge is almost two (1) miles long and the towers are (2) 746 feet tall.

③ Over one hundred sixty (1) thousand miles of (2) wire cable were used to construct the bridge.

④ Over four (1) hundred bridges were built by him (2) all over the world.

⑤ In conclusion, the Golden (1) Gate Bridge was a (2) great engineering success.

⑥ We were (1) very quiet and finally (2) it left.

⑦ It is 1, (1) 932 feet (2) deep and about 6 miles across.

⑧ This (1) explosion was heard, (2) and reported by the Native Americans.

⑨ Over five thousand square miles (1) were covered with (2) 6 inches of ash.

⑩ In conclusion, Crater Lake shows us the beauty of nature (1) and its incredible (2) power.

Now you try it. Listen and repeat. Put in the pauses.

This ∨Pause is a photograph of the Eiffel Tower.

2

It weighs seven ∨Pause thousand three hundred metric tons.

3

It was built in only ∨Pause 26 months and 3 days.

4

This is a photograph of ∨Pause me in front of Big Ben in London.

5

In London, I rode on the famous ∨Pause double decker buses.

6

The clock tower was completed in ∨Pause 1859.

Partner A

Partner A looks at this page. Partner B looks at page 82.

Practice 1 **Present this postcard to your partner! First, underline the key words. Then as you read, use stressing or pausing to emphasize those words.**

Greeting and Topic:

- Hello everybody.
- This is a postcard of the Eiffel Tower.

Tell your Story:

- I bought it in Paris last spring.
- I drank espresso at an outdoor cafe and ate freshly baked French bread for breakfast every morning.
- I went to the Louvre Museum and of course I saw the Eiffel Tower.

Tell its Story:

Present:

- The Eiffel Tower is over 320 meters high and it weighs seven thousand three hundred metric tons.

Past:

- It was designed by Alexendre-Gustave Eiffel.
- It was built for the World's Fair in 1889.
- Construction was started on January 26th, 1887.
- The Tower was completed on March 31st, 1889.
- It was built in only 26 months and 3 days.
- Only one-hundred-and twenty workers were needed to build the tower.

Closing:

- In conclusion, when the Eiffel Tower was completed it was the tallest man-made structure anywhere in the world. Even today it is the tallest structure in Paris.
- Thank you for listening.

Practice 2 **Listen to your partner and fill in the Fact File below:**

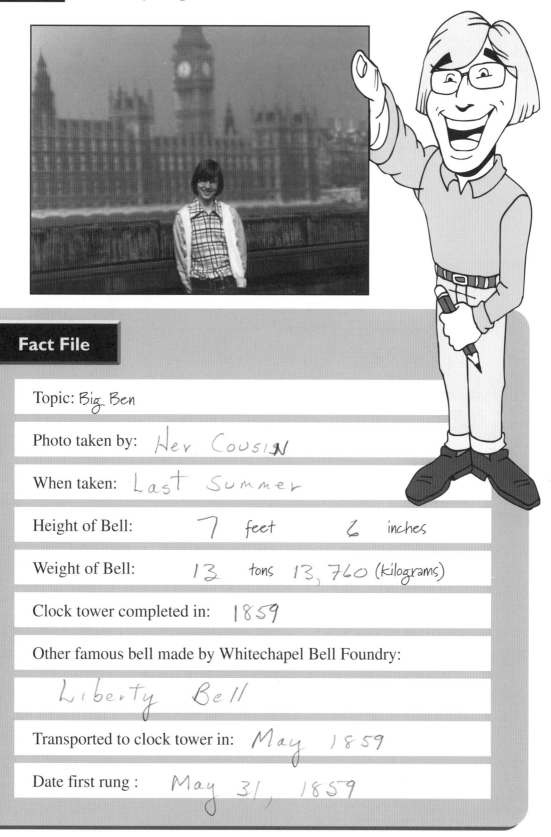

Fact File

Topic: Big Ben

Photo taken by: Her Cousin

When taken: Last Summer

Height of Bell: 7 feet 6 inches

Weight of Bell: 13 tons 13,760 (kilograms)

Clock tower completed in: 1859

Other famous bell made by Whitechapel Bell Foundry:

Liberty Bell

Transported to clock tower in: May 1859

Date first rung : May 31, 1859

Partner A looks at this page. Partner B looks at page 80.

Practice 1

Listen to your partner and fill in the Fact File below:

Fact File

Topic:	Eiffel Tower
Postcard bought in:	Paris
When bought:	last Spring
Height of Tower:	320 meters high
Weight of Tower:	7,300 metric Tons
Construction started:	Jan 26 1887
Construction finished:	Mar 31 1889
Construction period:	26 months 3 days
Number of workers needed:	120

Practice 2 **Present this photo to your partner! First, underline the key words. Then as you read, use stressing or pausing to emphasize those words.**

Greeting and Topic:

- Hi everybody.
- This is a photograph of me in front of Big Ben in London.

Tell your Story:

- It was taken by my cousin when I visited London last summer.
- In London, I drank tea at my aunt's house, went to a pub with my cousin, ate fish and chips and rode on the famous double-decker buses.
- I went to the Houses of Parliament and of course I saw Big Ben.

Tell its Story:

Present:

- Did you know that Big Ben is actually the name of the bell and not really the name of the clock tower?
- The bell is 7 feet 6 inches high, and weighs over 13 tons.
- That is 13,760 kilograms.

Past:

- The clock tower was completed in 1859.
- Big Ben was made by the Whitechapel Bell Foundry.
- The famous Liberty Bell in Philadelphia, Pennsylvania was also manufactured by the Whitechapel Bell Foundry.
- Big Ben was transported from Whitechapel Bell Foundry to the clock tower in May of 1859.
- All traffic was stopped and 16 horses were needed to pull the bell to the tower.
- The streets were lined with people and Big Ben was cheered as it passed. The bell was first rung on May 31st, 1859.

Closing:

- In conclusion, if you ever visit London be sure to visit the Houses of Parliament and listen to Big Ben.
- Thank you.

Use this pattern to make a show and tell speech about a postcard or photograph of your own:

Topic:

This is a postcard of • • •
This is a photograph of • • •

Tell your Story:

I bought it in • • •
• • • brought it to me from • • •
I found it • • •
This was given to me by • • •
This picture was taken by • • •
The weather was • • •
One night • • •
One day • • •

Tell its Story:

Present:

is	miles	long
are	feet	tall
	meters	high
	kilometers	wide
	yards	across
		deep
weighs	pounds	
	tons	
	kilograms	

Past:

was	built	during
were	started	in
	completed	by
	used	when
	designed	with
	formed	
	created	
	developed	
	discovered	

Closing:

In conclusion • • •

Make a show and tell speech!

Step 1 **CHOOSE**

Choose a postcard or a photograph of your own.

Step 2 **RESEARCH**

Research the subject at the library or on the internet.

Step 3 **WRITE**

Write the important facts about your subject in the Fact File below.

Step 4 **SPEAK**

Use your Fact File to give your own show and tell speech.

This is a ...

BEAUTIFUL HAWAII

Fact File

Topic:

Exercise 1 Choose the best verb to complete the sentence. The first one is done for you.

1. This (is/was/are/were) a model of the Space Needle.
2. I (buy/bought/was bought) this souvenir of the Space Needle in Seattle.
3. The Space Needle (is/was/are/were) 184 meters high.
4. It (build/built/was built) for the 1962 World's fair.
5. It (remodel/remodeled/was remodeled) recently.
6. The remodeling (complete/completed/was completed) in March 2001.

Exercise 2 Rewrite the following sentences using the passive form. The first one is done for you.

1. Leonardo da Vinci painted the famous Mona Lisa.
   The Mona Lisa was painted by Leonardo da Vinci.
2. He finished the painting in 1506.
   The painting was finished in 1506 .
3. The King of France purchased the painting from Leonardo.
   The painting was purchased from Leonardo by the K. of Fran .
4. King Louis the Fourteenth kept the painting in his palace.
   The painting was kept by K Louis XIV in his palace.
5. They moved the Mona Lisa to the Louvre Museum in 1793.
   The Mona Lisa was moved to the Louvre Museum in 1
6. An Italian painter stole the Mona Lisa from the Louvre on August 21, 1911.
   The Mona lisa was stolen from the Louvre on Aug 21 by an I
7. The police returned the painting to the Louvre two years later.
   The painting was returned to the Louvre two years la by the police

~ Award Presentations ~

Presenting & Accepting Awards

ABOUT THIS UNIT

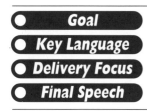

Goal	Learn to present and accept awards and certificates
Key Language	She participated in ~ She has spoken at ~
Delivery Focus	Gesture practice
Final Speech	Present and accept a certificate of excellence

Listen to the following Award Presentation and Award Acceptance speeches. Check the best answers. The first one is done for you.

1 Who is being introduced?

- ❑ Judy Garland
- ☑ Jody Williams
- ❑ Venus Williams

2 What has Jody won?

- ❑ 1957 Nobel Prize for Peace
- ❑ 1997 Nobel Prize for Physics
- ☑ 1997 Nobel Prize for Peace

3 Where did Jody receive her Master's Degree?

- ❑ The International English School in Mexico
- ☑ The School for International Training
- ❑ The School for English Training

4 Where has Jody spoken?

- ❑ at the White House and Congress
- ✓❑ at the United Nations and European Parliament
- ❑ at the United States Senate and British Parliament

5 Where has Jody taught English?

- ☑ in Mexico, the U.K. and Washington, D.C.
- ❑ in the United Nations and the European Parliament
- ❑ in the School for International Training

6 Who does Jody thank in her Acceptance Speech?

- ❑ everyone at the Campaign to Ban Landmines
- ☑ everyone at The School for International Training
- ❑ everyone at home especially, Mom and Dad

Listen to the following Award Presentation and Award Acceptance speeches.
Check the best answers.

① Who is being introduced?

☑ Ms. Reiko Okano
❑ Ms. Seiko Matsuda
❑ Ms. Chidori Ando

② How long has she played golf?

❑ only a few years
☑ only two years
❑ since New Year's

③ What has she done recently?

❑ made a goal
❑ hit a grand slam
☑ made a hole in one

④ Where has she played golf?

❑ Hawaii, Taiwan, and Korea
❑ Hawaii, Palm Beach, and North Korea
☑ Hawaii, Guam, and Korea

⑤ What tournament did she recently participate in?

❑ The All Japan Professional Golf Tournament
❑ The All Japan Pro Wrestling Tournament
☑ The All Japan High School Golf Tournament

⑥ Who does she thank in her Acceptance Speech?

❑ her golf coach
❑ her golf clubs
❑ her tennis coach

Study these expressions for award presentation speeches.

Introduction:	**This morning I would like you to welcome** Jody Williams. **Today, we would like to honor** our classmate, Ms. Reiko Okano
Who are they?:	Jody **is the coordinator of** the International Campaign to Ban Landmines. She **is a member of** the school golf team.
What have they done?:	She **won** the 1997 Nobel Prize for Peace. She **has spoken** at the United Nations and at the European Parliament. She **recently made** a hole in one. She **participated in** the All Japan High School Golf Tournament last month. She **has played golf** in Hawaii, Guam, and Korea.
Point of Interest:	**You may be surprised to learn that** Jody is also an English teacher. She **received** a Masters Degree in teaching English **from** the School for International Training in 1984. She **has taught** English in Mexico, the UK, and Washington DC. **What is amazing is that** she has played golf for only 2 years.
Welcoming:	**Please welcome,** Jody Williams. **Let's give** her **a warm welcome.**
Presentation of Award:	Jody**, on behalf of** this school, **I would like to present you with this certificate for** your excellent work to ban landmines. Ms. Okano**, it is my great pleasure to give you this award for excellence** in golf.

Acceptance

Study these expressions for award acceptance speeches.

Greeting:	**Thank you, ladies and gentlemen.** **Thank you very much, everyone.**
Expressing Appreciation:	**I am truly honored to receive this** certificate. **I am really grateful for this** award.
Special Thanks:	**I'd like to thank everyone at** the School for International Training **for their** inspiration. **I'd like to thank** my golf coach **for** all his help.
Future:	**I hope you will continue to support** the Campaign to Ban Landmines. **I will try my best to improve** my golf game in the future.
Repeated Thanks:	**Again, this certificate/award/trophy/medal means a lot to me.** **Thank you very much.** **Once again, this is a great honor.** **Thank you again.**

Practice 1 **Partner A looks at this page. Partner B doesn't need a book. Read these words. Partner B repeats and adds gestures.**

① Big

② Pull

③ Long

④ Round

⑤ On the top

⑥ On the left side

⑦ My first point is

⑧ It is the widest river.

⑨ Turn the key to the right.

⑩ It is nearly 300 meters tall.

⑪ First, pour the water into the cup.

⑫ Next, add ice and stir with a spoon.

⑬ The movie can be divided into 3 parts.

⑭ (Think of your own)

⑮ (Think of your own)

⑯ (Think of your own)

Practice 2 **Partner B looks at this page. Partner A doesn't need a book. Read these words. Partner A repeats and adds gestures.**

① Push

② Short

③ Small

④ Square

⑤ On the bottom

⑥ Open the door

⑦ On the right side

⑧ The second step is

⑨ It is the deepest lake.

⑩ It is almost 2 miles long.

⑪ The book has 4 sections.

⑫ First, lift the top and put in the soap.

⑬ Second, close the lid and push the start button.

⑭ (Think of your own)

⑮ (Think of your own)

⑯ (Think of your own)

Partner B

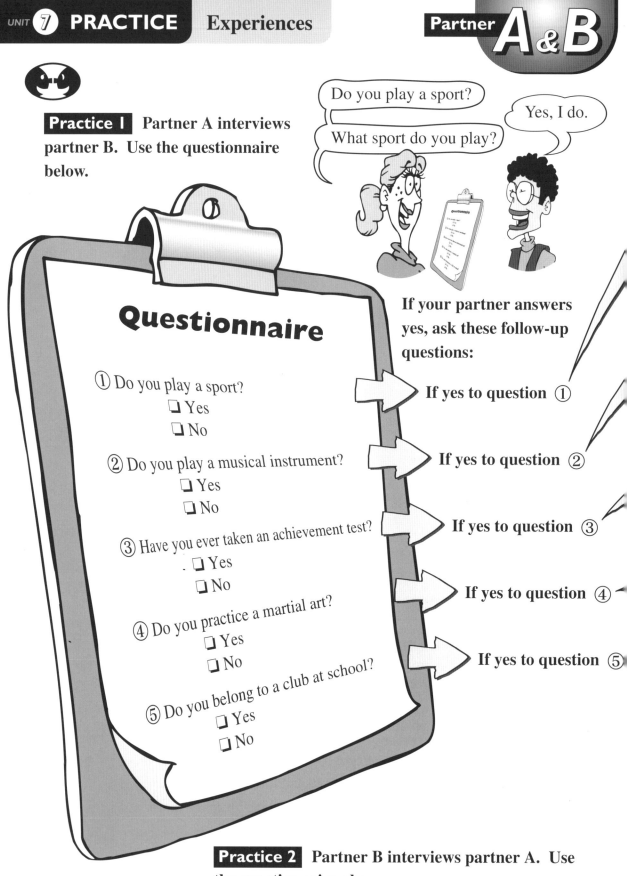

Partner A & B

Practice 1 Partner A interviews partner B. Use the questionnaire below.

Do you play a sport?
What sport do you play?
Yes, I do.

Questionnaire

① Do you play a sport?
❑ Yes
❑ No

② Do you play a musical instrument?
❑ Yes
❑ No

③ Have you ever taken an achievement test?
❑ Yes
❑ No

④ Do you practice a martial art?
❑ Yes
❑ No

⑤ Do you belong to a club at school?
❑ Yes
❑ No

If your partner answers yes, ask these follow-up questions:

If yes to question ①

If yes to question ②

If yes to question ③

If yes to question ④

If yes to question ⑤

Practice 2 Partner B interviews partner A. Use the questionnaire above.

Follow-up questions--write your answers on the lines below.

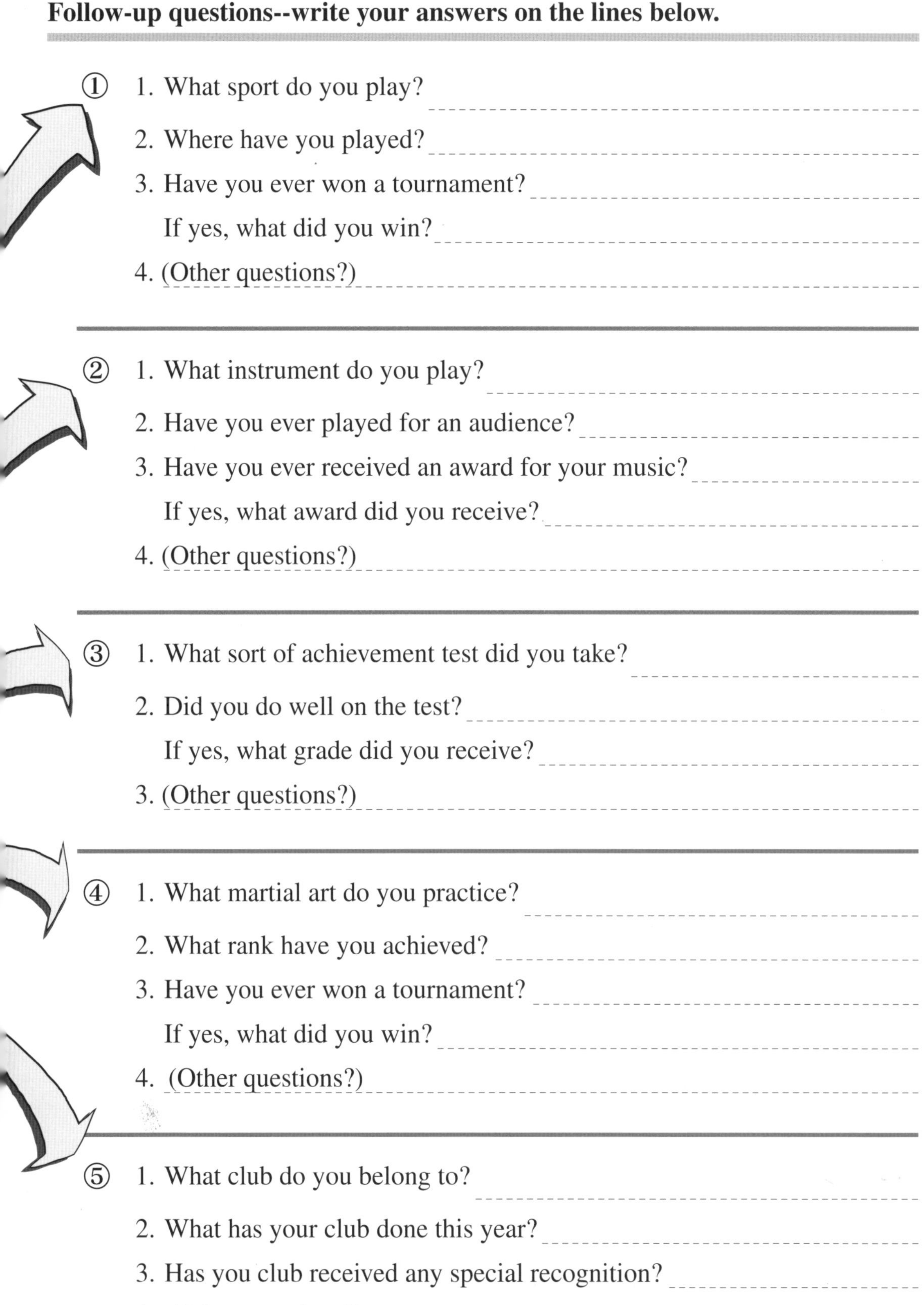

① 1. What sport do you play? ______

2. Where have you played? ______

3. Have you ever won a tournament? ______

If yes, what did you win? ______

4. (Other questions?) ______

② 1. What instrument do you play? ______

2. Have you ever played for an audience? ______

3. Have you ever received an award for your music? ______

If yes, what award did you receive? ______

4. (Other questions?) ______

③ 1. What sort of achievement test did you take? ______

2. Did you do well on the test? ______

If yes, what grade did you receive? ______

3. (Other questions?) ______

④ 1. What martial art do you practice? ______

2. What rank have you achieved? ______

3. Have you ever won a tournament? ______

If yes, what did you win? ______

4. (Other questions?) ______

⑤ 1. What club do you belong to? ______

2. What has your club done this year? ______

3. Has you club received any special recognition? ______

4. (Other questions?) ______

Select from these phrases to make an award presentation speech:

Introduction:	**This morning I would like you to welcome • • •** **Today, we would like to honor, • • •**
Who are they?:	**• • • is the coordinator/president/captain/of • • •** **• • • is a member of • • •**
What have they done?:	**• • • won • • •** **• • • has spoken • • •** **• • • recently made • • •** **• • • participated in • • •** **• • • has played golf/tennis/baseball/shogi • • •**
Point of Interest:	**You may be surprised to learn that • • •** **• • • received • • • from • • •** **• • • has taught • • •** **What is amazing is that • • •**
Welcoming:	**Please welcome, • • •** **Let's give • • • a warm welcome.**
Presentation of Award:	**• • •, on behalf of • • •, I would like to present you with this certificate for • • •** **• • •, it is my great pleasure to give you this award for excellence • • •**

Acceptance

Select from these phrases to make an award acceptance speech:

Greeting:	**Thank you, ladies and gentlemen.** **Thank you very much, everyone**
Expressing Appreciation:	**I am truly honored to receive this •••** **I am really grateful for this •••**
Special Thanks:	**I'd like to thank everyone at ••• for their •••** **I'd like to thank ••• for •••**
Future:	**I hope you will continue to support •••** **I will try my best to improve •••**
Repeated Thanks:	**Again, this certificate/award/trophy/medal means a lot to me.** **Thank you very much.** **Once again, this is a great honor.** **Thank you.**

Prepare for your final award presentation speech:

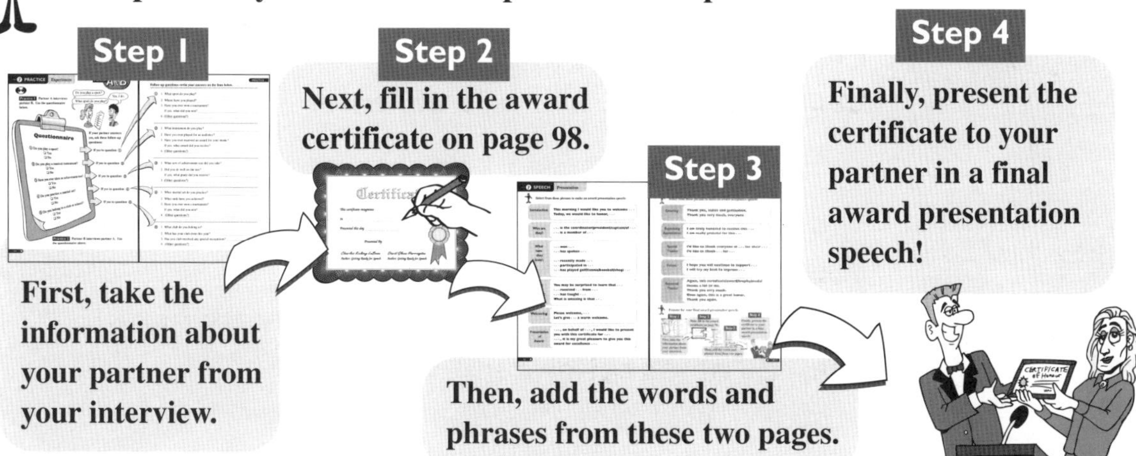
Step 1
First, take the information about your partner from your interview.
Step 2
Next, fill in the award certificate on page 98.
Step 3
Then, add the words and phrases from these two pages.
Step 4
Finally, present the certificate to your partner in a final award presentation speech!

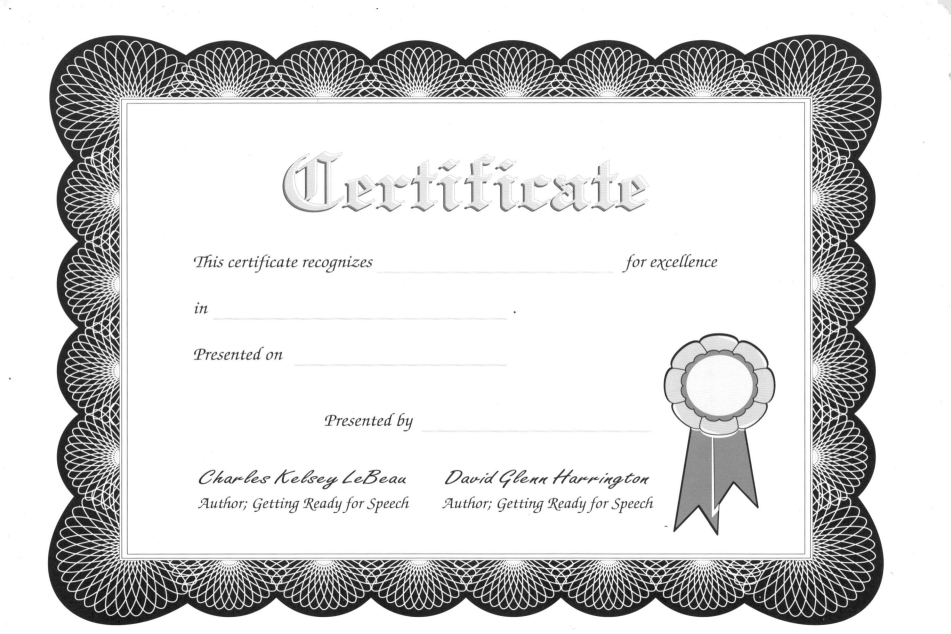

Certificate

This certificate recognizes ______________________ for excellence

in ______________________.

Presented on ______________________

Presented by ______________________

Charles Kelsey LeBeau	*David Glenn Harrington*
Author; Getting Ready for Speech	Author; Getting Ready for Speech